Project Explore

Starter

Student's Book

Sarah Phillips
Paul Shipton

OXFORD
UNIVERSITY PRESS

Based on an original concept
by Tom Hutchinson

CW00742628

Contents

Contents ③

Introduction

Lily Finn Sid Chris

A Lily and Finn

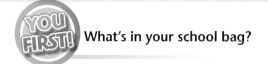 **YOU FIRST!** What's in your school bag?

1 a 🔊 **1.02** ▶ Read and listen to the story. What is in Lily's school bag?

1 pencil
2 ____
5 ____
7 notebook
9 scissors
10 ____
12 ____
11 pencil case
3 ruler
4 sharpener
6 crayon
8 ____

Put your books in your school bags!

OK, Mum.

Yes, Mum.

Finished!

What's that?

That? It's a ruler.

It isn't a ruler! It's Chris! Go to your cage!

Bye, Mum.

Goodbye! Have a good day!

Hi Jake.

What are these, Lily?

Oh! They're pencils.

Wait a minute! They aren't in your bag now.

Open your bag, Lily!

Oh! What's that? Is it a snake?

Yes, it is. It's Sid!

b Read the story again. Are the sentences true (T) or false (F)?

1 Finn and Lily are brother and sister.
2 Chris is a ruler.
3 Sid is a snake.
4 Chris isn't in Lily's bag.
5 Sid is in the bag.

Vocabulary

2 a Complete the labels in exercise 1 with the words in the box.

> book calculator pen rubber school bag

b 🔊 **1.03** Listen and check, then repeat.

Look!

pencil → pencils   book → books

Grammar and Speaking

be: it is/they are

3 Look at the story again. Match the sentence halves.

1 It's   a pencils.
2 It isn't   b a ruler.
3 They're   c in your bag now.
4 They aren't   d a ruler.

It's a book.

It **isn't** a chameleon.

They're books.

They **aren't** snakes.

It + **is** = It's
They + **are** = They're

4 a Get ready to speak **Complete the dialogues.**

Is it a calculator?

No, it isn't! ___ a book!

Are they crayons?

No, they aren't! ___ pencils!

b 🔊 **1.04** Listen and check.

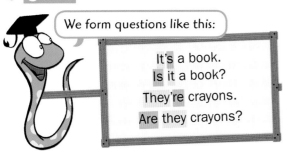

We form questions like this:

It's a book.
Is it a book?
They're crayons.
Are they crayons?

c Work with a partner. Play the *Draw and Guess* game like Chris and Sid. Change the **highlighted** words.

Vocabulary

5 a Complete the labels with the words in the box.

black   orange   pink   red   white

12 brown

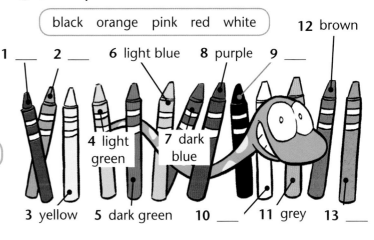

1 ___   2 ___   6 light blue   8 purple   9 ___

4 light green   7 dark blue

3 yellow   5 dark green   10 ___   11 grey   13 ___

b 🔊 **1.05** Listen and check, then repeat.

c Say your three favourite colours.

My favourite colours are red, orange and blue.

d Over to you! Work with a partner. Play the *What's Missing?* game.

6 a Look at the first picture in exercise 1. Complete the dialogue.

A   What colour is it? | B   No, it isn't.
B   It's red and blue. | A   Is it the ___ ?
A   Is it the sharpener? | B   Yes, it is.

b 🔊 **1.06** Listen and check.

c Work with a partner. Play the *Guessing game.* Change the **highlighted** words.

Everyday English Imperatives

7 a Find the instructions in this unit. Which exercises are they for?

1 Read and listen.   1a
2 Match the sentence halves.   ___
3 Work with a partner.   ___
4 Find the instructions.   ___
5 Complete the dialogue.   ___
6 Play the *Draw and Guess* game.   ___
7 Listen and check.   ___

b 🔊 **1.07** Listen and repeat.

c Work with a partner. Play the *Miming game.*
Student **A** mimes a verb.
Student **B** says the verb.

EXTRA   Write about the things in your pencil case.

e.g.: My pencils are blue and black.

B New friends

 What things can you ask a new friend?

1 **Match the numbers to the words.**

9   3   7   6   10   1   4   8   5   2

a one   **b** two   **c** three   **d** four   **e** five
f six   **g** seven   **h** eight   **i** nine   **j** ten

b **Match the numbers to the words in the box.**

> fifteen   eleven   thirteen
> fourteen   nineteen   seventeen
> sixteen   twenty   twelve   eighteen

2 **a** **Find the numbers 11–20 in the photos.**

c ◀) **1.08** **Listen and repeat.**

3 **a** ◀) **1.09** ▶ **Read and listen to the story.**
Where do the new friends meet?

Rosie   Sorry!
Leila   I'm Leila. What's your name?
Rosie   Hi! My name's Rosie and this is my brother, Joel.
Jan   My name's Jan.
Joel   Where are you from, Jan?
Jan   I'm Polish.
Rosie   What about you, Leila?
Leila   I'm from Scotland, but we live in Oxford now.

Rosie   How old are you?
Jan   I'm 11.
Rosie   Me too! Great! We're in Year 6 together.
Jan   How old is Joel?
Rosie   He's 13. He's in Year 8.
Jan   Look! That's the bus. Run!

Leila   What's your favourite film, Joel?
Joel   I like Star Wars.
Leila   Me too. Do you like R2-D2?
Joel   Yes, I do! Who's your favourite character?
Leila   Chewbacca. Look, he's on my bag.
Joel   I don't like Chewbacca. My favourite is Darth Vader!

Jan   Oh no!
Rosie   Excuse me, can you phone my mum, please?
Mrs Rowe   Yes, of course. What's her phone number?
Rosie   It's 0174 362895.
Mrs Rowe   Here you are.
Rosie   Hi Mum! It's Rosie.
Mum   Are you OK?
Rosie   Yes, we're fine. But we missed the bus! Can you take us to school?
Mum   I don't believe it! On your first day!

b Read the story again. Answer the questions about the story.

1 Who are brother and sister?

2 Who is from Poland?

3 Who is from Scotland?

4 Who is in Year 8?

Everyday English Likes

4 a Read the story again. Copy and complete the table.

⊕	⊖	❓
I 🙂 Star Wars.	I 🙁 Chewbacca.	___ R2-D2?

b Get ready to speak Complete the dialogue with colours.

Do you like ▪ ?

No, I don't.

Yes, I do. Do you like ▪ ?

c 🔊 1.10 Listen and check.

d Over to you! Talk to your classmates. Find two likes you have in common.

5 a Find the questions in the story.

We ask these questions to find out about another person.

1 What's your name?

2 Where are you from, Jan?

3 How old are you?

4 What's your favourite film?

5 Who's your favourite character?

6 What's her phone number?

b Match the answers to the questions in exercise 5a.

You can use these answers to give information about you.

a I'm 11.

b My name's Jan.

c I'm from Poland.

d It's 0174 362895.

e It's Star Wars.

f R2-D2.

Vocabulary and Listening

6 a Match the countries (1–12) to the nationalities (a–l).

I'm from India. I'm Indian.

I'm from Spain. I'm Spanish.

1 England	a Czech
2 Scotland	b Hungarian
3 Ireland	c Irish
4 Wales	d Indian
5 Hungary	e Welsh
6 Croatia	f Croatian
7 Serbia	g Chinese
8 Slovenia	h Serbian
9 Czech Republic	i Slovenian
10 China	j Scottish
11 Spain	k English
12 India	l Spanish

b 🔊 1.11 Listen and check, then repeat.

7 a 🔊 1.12 Listen to the dialogues. Where are Tilly and Prakesh from?

b 🔊 1.12 Copy the table into your notebook. Listen again and complete.

	Tilly	Prakesh
Age		
Favourite book	*The Hobbit*	
Favourite team		Olympiacos

Speaking

8 Get ready to speak Write the questions the teacher asked Tilly in exercise 7.

9 Work with a partner. Ask the questions in exercise 7. Answer them for you. You can ask about likes, too.

What's your favourite book?

It's *Matilda*.

EXTRA How many English words can you write starting with these letters?

E N G L I S H

England, eleven, eight...

YOU FIRST! How many verbs can you say in English in one minute?

Vocabulary

1 **a** Complete the labels with the words in the box.

> play football   play the guitar   sing   swim

b 🔊 **1.13** Listen and check, then repeat.

c Work in small groups. Play the *I Say* game.

1 Copy the picture into your notebook.

2 Listen to your teacher's instructions.

3 Play the game and shoot a basket.

I say swim!   I say don't run.   Rollerblade!

Reading and Grammar

2 **a** Look at the photos. Who is the conversation between?

b Read the messages. Who are the sentences about?

1 She's in the park.

2 She isn't in the park.

3 She's in a wheelchair.

4 Basketball is her favourite game.

1 play basketball

P-O-L-L-Y!

3 ___   4 run   2 spell

7 climb a tree

6 ride a bike

5 ___

8 walk

9 draw

11 rollerblade

10 speak Chinese

12 ___

13 ___

c Read the conversation again. Then match the sentence halves.

1 Leila can't   a play basketball.

2 Leila can   b walk.

3 Leila can't   c rollerblade.

d 🔊 **1.14** Listen and check, then repeat.

We make sentences with **can** like this.

I can climb trees.

I can't play the guitar.

e Over to you! Write sentences about what you *can* and *can't* do. Use the phrases in exercise 1.

I can swim.
I can't rollerblade.

Hi Leila! I'm in the park. Can you come and rollerblade with me?

Sorry! I can't rollerblade.

Why not?

Look! I'm in a wheelchair. My leg is broken.

Can you walk?

No, I can't. But I can play basketball!

Really?

Yes, really! My chair is very fast!

Great! We can play basketball. It's my favourite game.

Fantastic! I love basketball. See you soon!

Speaking

3 Get ready to speak Prepare three questions to ask your friends. Think of answers to your questions.

We make questions with **can** like this.
I **can** play basketball.
Can you play basketball?

4 Ask your friends your questions. Can you find three people who give the same answers as you?

Can you play the guitar?

No, I can't.   Yes, I can.

Pronunciation   The alphabet

5 a 🔊 **1.15** Listen and repeat.

A H J K	B C D E G P T V
F L M N S X	Z	I Y	O
Q U W	R

b Why are the letters in these groups?

c Spell your name to your partner.

d Work with a partner. Play the *Spelling game*. Student **A** starts spelling a word from this unit. Student **B** guesses the word.

R – E...
     I know. Red.

No. R – E – A...
     I know! Read.

Study tip!

Keep a vocabulary book. Practise spelling new words!

Listening and Speaking

6 a 🔊 **1.16** Listen and match the dialogues (1–4) to the pictures (a–d).

a

8?

b

Open your books at page four.
???

c

Robot?

d

?   Sarah.

b Get ready to speak Match the questions (1–4) to the answers (a–d).

1 Excuse me. What does 'robot' mean?
2 Can you spell '8', please?
3 Can you say that again, please?
4 How do you say your name in English?

a You say 'Sarah'.
b Open your books at page four.
c It means 'robot'!
d E-I-G-H-T.

7 Work with a partner. Practise the dialogues. You can change the highlighted words.

 EXTRA Find five words in this unit that are difficult to spell. Practise spelling them.

1 Me!

1A In the playground

 YOU FIRST! How many things can you say about yourself in one minute?

Vocabulary and Grammar *be*: singular forms

1 a Complete the labels with the words in the box.

cold   happy   hot   sad

picture A

Adam
1 scared

Mrs Collins
2 angry

Rafael
4 hungry

Mr Kovács
3 tired

Dylan
6 ___

Sandra
5 excited

Lara
10 ___

Karina
9 bored

Duncan
7 ___

Myra
8 ___

Agata
11 thirsty

b ▶ **1.17** Listen and check, then repeat.

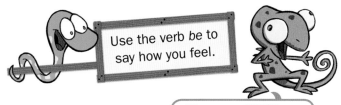

Use the verb *be* to say how you feel.

I'm happy. I'm not sad.

c Make three true sentences about how you feel now.

I'm not hungry.   I'm sleepy.

This is how you make questions.

I am hungry.
Are you hungry?

Yes, I am.   No, I'm not.

d ▶ **1.18** Listen and repeat the dialogues.

A Are you hungry?
B No, I'm not.
A Me neither!

A Are you tired?
B Yes, I am.
A Me too!

e Over to you! Ask your friends the questions in exercise 1d. Change the highlighted words. Can you find three students with the same answers as you?

Study tip!

You learn to speak English by speaking English. Practise in class and at home. You can record sentences on a phone or tablet.

▶ **Workbook** page 2, exercises 1–4

2 Read the sentences. Then match the words (1–2) to the pictures (a–b).

> Look at **Dylan**. **He's** sad.

> Look at **Karina**. **She's** bored.

a   b

1 He   2 She

3 Read the puzzles. Write the names of the people from the picture in exercise 1.

1 He's scared. He isn't 11; he's ten.
   He's from England.   Adam

2 She's eight. She's happy. She isn't
   from Spain; she's from India.   ____

3 He's Hungarian. He isn't a student;
   he's a teacher. He's tired.   ____

4 She isn't hungry; she's thirsty.
   She's from Poland. She's nine.   ____

> **Am**, **are** and **is** are singular forms of the verb **be**.

Remember!

> *Singular* means one person or one thing.

4 a Complete the sentences about Rafael and Lara. Use *He's*, *She's*, *He isn't* or *She isn't*.

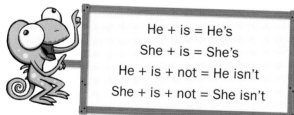

> He + is = He's
> She + is = She's
> He + is + not = He isn't
> She + is + not = She isn't

Rafael
1 He's from Spain.
2 ____ from Slovenia.
3 ____ hungry.

Lara
4 ____ Croatian.
5 ____ tired.
6 ____ cold.

b 📝 Write true sentences and three false sentences about two other people in the picture in exercise 1a. Use the examples in exercise 4a to help you.

c Work with a partner. Swap sentences. Are your partner's sentences true or false?

▶ **Workbook** page 3, exercises 5–7

Speaking

5 a Get ready to speak Look at picture A in exercise 1 and picture B below. Complete the dialogue with *A* or *B*.

> She's angry.
> Is she angry?

> Yes, she is.

> No, she isn't.

picture B

Agata
Duncan
Adam
Rafael
Sandra
Lara
Myra
Karina
Dylan
Mrs Collins
Mr Kovács

> Is Myra tired?

> No, she isn't. She's happy.

> I know. It's picture ____!

> You're right.

b 🔊 **1.19** Listen and check, then repeat.

6 Work with a partner. Play the *Guess the Person* game. Use the dialogue in exercise 5 to help you.

EXTRA Draw and label emojis for the words in exercise 1.

1B My family

Is your family big or small?

Vocabulary

1 a Look at the family picture. How many pairs of twins can you see?

b Complete the labels with the words in the box.

brother   father   mother   sister

5 aunt
1 grandmother
2 grandfather
3 ___
4 ___
7 ___
9 cousins
6 uncle
8 ___
me

c 🔊 **1.20** Listen and check, then repeat.

2 a 🔊 **1.21** Listen and repeat.

twenty   thirty   forty   fifty   sixty

seventy   eighty   ninety   one hundred

b Add five more numbers to the series.
21, 32, 43,...

c 🔊 **1.22** Listen and check.

3 a Look at the family in exercise 1.
Complete the dialogue with a family member.

A How old is she? | B No.
B She's 36. | A The ___ .
A The ___ . | B That's right.

b 🔊 **1.23** Listen and check.

4 Over to you! Work with a partner. Ask and answer about the people in the family picture.

▶ **Workbook** page 4, exercise 1

Reading

5 a Read the descriptions (1–5) and choose the correct family photo (a–e) from page 13.

My family album

1 ___ This is my brother. We're twins; we're 11 years old. We aren't identical twins. My brother is tall and strong. I'm tall, too, but I'm not strong.

2 ___ My mum and my aunt are twins. They're 35 years old. They are identical twins. They're short and pretty.

3 ___ My dad and my uncle are twins. They're 42 years old. They aren't identical. My dad is tall and my uncle is short. They are very clever!

4 ___ My cousins are twins, too. They're very young. They're one year old. Are they identical? We don't know! I think all babies are identical!

5 ___ My grandparents are 75. They're old! My grandfather is very nice. He can play the guitar, he can sing, and he loves animals.

a  b c

1 ___ 2 ___ 3 ___ 4 ___ 5 ___

d e

6 ___ 7 ___ 8 ___

b Label the people with the **highlighted** words in exercise 5a.

Study tip!

Look carefully at the pictures in the book. They help you understand new words.

> **Workbook** page 4, exercise 2

Grammar *be*: plural forms

6 Look at exercise 5a again. Match the words (1–2) to the pictures (a–b).

1 We 2 They

7 a Copy the table into your notebook. Complete the table with the plural forms of the verb *be*.

	➕	➖	❓
we			
you	*are* / *'re*		Are you...?
they			

 *You are* is the singular and plural form!

b Are the sentences true (T) or false (F) for you? Correct the false sentences. Use the pronouns *I, she, we, he* and *they* in your answers.

1 I'm a twin.
2 My friend and I are 11.
3 My brother isn't strong.
4 My aunt and uncle are tall.
5 My grandmother and grandfather aren't old.
6 My friend and I are short.

c Answer the questions.

1 Are your mother and father English?
2 Is your mother short?
3 Are your friends old?
4 Is your teacher tall?

d Over to you! Think of four questions to ask the other students about their friends and family. Use the questions in exercise 7c to help you.

e Ask your classmates. Can you find three things you have in common with other students?

> **Workbook** pages 4–5, exercises 3–5

Writing

8 Get ready to write Write the names of four people in your family. Then add more information.

a Who is he or she?
b How old is he or she?
c Describe the person.
e.g.: Michael – brother – 10 – English – short and fair

> **Workbook** page 5, exercises 6–7

9 Write about your family. You can draw a picture or add a photo, too. Use the example to help you.

These are my brothers, Michael and James. Michael is 10; James is 12. Michael is short. James isn't short; he's tall. They're cold in this photo. They aren't happy!

EXTRA Draw and label your family tree.

YOU FIRST! What months do you know in English?

1 a 🔊 1.24 ▶ Read and listen to the story. Where are the cake decorations?

b Read the story again. Are the sentences true (T) or false (F)? Correct the false sentences.

1 Finn is happy.
2 Pictures of Lily and Finn are on the birthday cake.
3 Chris's favourite colour is green.
4 Some friends are at the door.

5 The children are hungry.
6 The children follow Mum.
7 Sid is angry with Chris.

Vocabulary

2 a Put the dates in the correct order.

31st December

3rd March

23rd September

21st July

5th May 4th April

1st January 26th October

2nd February

27th November 22nd August 20th June

b 🔊 **1.25** Listen and check.

c Now say the dates in the correct order.

1st, 2nd, 3rd, etc. are called **ordinal numbers**.

3 Over to you! **Ask your friends about their birthdays. How many people have the same birthday month as you?**

When's your birthday?

It's the 23rd of September.

▶ **Workbook** page 6, exercise 1

Grammar Possessives

4 a **Look at the story again. Complete the sentences.**

1 It's my birthday!

2 ___ birthday? It's ___ birthday!

3 ___ cake is finished!

4 Green is ___ favourite colour.

5 ___ tummy is spotty.

The missing words are **possessives**.

I'm three.
My birthday is on the 1st of April.

He's four.
His birthday is on the 2nd of May.

b **Match the subject pronouns (1–8) to the possessives (a–h).**

1 you 2 I 3 they 4 she 5 it 6 he 7 we 8 you

a his b your c her d our e its f their g my h your

You can substitute *his*, *her* or *their* with a name + *'s*.
It's **their** birthday. = It's **Lily and Finn's** birthday.

5 Complete the sentences with *his*, *her* or *their*.

1 This is Finn's present. = This is his present.

2 This is Lily's present. = This is ___ present.

3 This is Chris and Sid's present. = This is ___ present.

▶ **Workbook** pages 6–7, exercises 2–5

Pronunciation

6 a 🔊 **1.26** **Listen and clap the rhythm.**

○ ○ ○ ○
When's his birthday?   When's her birthday?
The 2nd of June.   The 3rd of May.
The 2nd of June.   The 3rd of May.
That's very soon.   Oh, that's today!

b 🔊 **1.27** **Mark the rhythm with circles. Listen and check, then repeat.**

▶ **Workbook** page 7, exercise 6

Listening and Speaking

7 🔊 **1.28** **Listen to Tom and Eva. Then complete the sentences with *Tom's*, *Eva's* or *Tom and Eva's*.**

YOUR FAVOURITES!

1 ___ birthday is in March.

2 ___ birthday is in July.

3 ___ favourite colour is blue.

4 ___ favourite game is Karts!

5 ___ favourite number is ten.

6 ___ favourite food is pizza.

7 ___ lucky number is 29.

8 Get ready to speak **Choose two of your classmates and think of three or four sentences about them.**

9 **Tell your classmates about other students in the class. Can they guess their names?**

Her favourite colour is blue. Her birthday is in June. Her sister is in Year 8. What's her name?

 EXTRA **Write two true sentences and two false sentences about you. Swap sentences with a partner. Can they guess the false sentences?**

What's your favourite day at school?

1 a 🔊 **1.29** ▶ **Read and listen to the story.**

1

Joel It's Tuesday tomorrow! Fantastic! I've got Maths and Art. They're my favourite subjects!

Dad What about you, Rosie?

Rosie I don't like Art, but I've got Science. I love Science.

Dad Are your bags ready for PE?

Rosie Yes, I've got my gymnastics kit.

Joel And I've got my football kit.

Dad Great.

2

Joel What time is it?

Dad It's half past eight.

Rosie Half past eight! We're late.

Joel Why? What time's the bus?

Rosie It's at half past eight!

Dad Run!

b Read the story again. Answer the questions.

1 Are Rosie and Joel's bags ready?

2 Are they late for the bus?

3 Is Rosie at a football class?

4 What's Joel's problem?

3

Leila Hey Joel, where's Rosie?

Joel She's at gymnastics. Her class is at quarter to three.

Leila What about your football training?

Joel It's at three o'clock.

Jan Well, it's five to three now. Run!

4

Trainer Are you ready, Joel?

Joel Nearly.

Trainer Well, hurry up!

Joel Oh no!

Trainer What's the matter?

Joel This is my sister's bag. Look! I can't play football today.

Vocabulary

2 a Complete the timetable with the words in the box.

| Art | English | History | Maths | Music |
| PE | Science | Spanish | Technology |

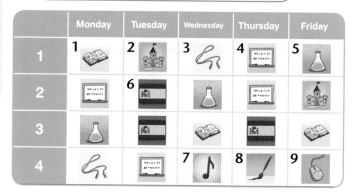

	Monday	Tuesday	Wednesday	Thursday	Friday
1	1	2	3	4	5
2		6			
3					
4			7	8	9

b 🔊 **1.30** **Listen and check, then repeat.**

c What are your top three subjects at school?

d Talk to your classmates. Can you find a friend with the same top three subjects as you?

> Do you like Maths?

> Yes, I do. What about you?

▶ **Workbook** page 8, exercise 1

Everyday English

3 a Look at the story again. Match the sentence halves.

1 The bus is at
2 Rosie's gymnastics class is at
3 Joel's football training is at

a three o'clock.
b half past eight.
c quarter to three.

> We say times like this.

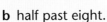

b Put the clocks in the correct order.

a three o'clock   b quarter to four   c five past three

d twenty-five to four   e quarter past three   f half past three

g five to four

c 🔊 **1.31** Listen and check, then repeat.

> You can say the time in two different ways.

half past ten = ten thirty

quarter to eleven = ten forty-five

d Find two questions about time in the story.

4 a Put the days of the week in the correct order.

Friday   Monday   Wednesday   Saturday   Tuesday   Sunday   Thursday

b 🔊 **1.32** Listen and check, then repeat.

c Ask and answer about your timetable.

▶ **Workbook** page 8, exercises 2–4

Listening

5 a 🔊 **1.33** Listen and answer the questions.

1 Which is Joel's favourite day?   Tuesday
2 Which is Rosie's favourite day?
3 Which is Jan's favourite day?

b 🔊 **1.33** Listen again and answer the questions about the three children.

Joel
1 What time is History?
2 What time is PE?

Rosie
1 What time is Science?
2 Are Science and Music Joel's favourite subjects?

Jan
1 What time is Music?
2 Is Art after lunch?

c Complete the dialogue.

Jan   What's your favourite day at school?
Joel   ¹Tuesday.
Jan   Why?
Joel   I've got Maths at ²___ . I love Maths.
Jan   Me too.
Joel   I've got ³___ at quarter to ten, and then I've got Art. They're great!
Jan   I don't like ⁴___ . History is OK.
Joel   I've got ⁵___ at quarter to twelve. And I've got chess after lunch! It's a brilliant day!

d 🔊 **1.34** Listen and check.

Look!

You can talk about your timetable like this.
I've got Biology at half past nine.

Speaking

6 Get ready to speak What are your answers to Jan's questions in exercise 5c? Make some notes.

7 Tell your classmates about your favourite day at school. Can you find someone with the same favourite day as you?

 EXTRA Draw four clocks with different times. Swap with a partner. Say the times.

Story

Read the puzzle on page 9 of the Workbook and do the exercises.

Vocabulary and Grammar

1 a Label the photos with family member names.

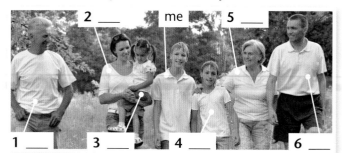

2 ___   me   5 ___

1 ___   3 ___   4 ___   6 ___

7 ___

8 cousin   9 ___

b Complete the descriptions of the father and the grandmother in the photo using the words in the box.

old   pretty   short   strong   tall   young

1 The father *is tall* and ___ .
2 The grandmother ___ .

2 a Write about the smileys. Use the words in the box.

bored   cold   excited   ~~happy~~   hot   scared

Tom and Tony

Polly and Peter

1 They aren't happy.   2 ___

Sue

Bob

3 ___   4 ___   5 ___   6 ___

b Put the words in the correct order to make questions. Then answer them.

1 Are   happy   Tom and Tony   ?   ___
2 Sue   Is   angry   ?   ___
3 cold   Is   Bob   ?   ___
4 Polly and Peter   excited   Are   ?   ___

3 Complete the table with personal pronouns or the possessive.

I		he				we	you	
	your			her	its			their

4 a Choose the correct words to complete the text.

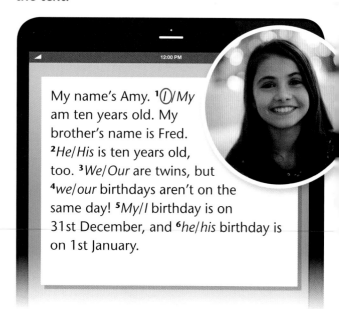

12:00 PM

My name's Amy. **1**(*I*)/*My* am ten years old. My brother's name is Fred. **2***He*/*His* is ten years old, too. **3***We*/*Our* are twins, but **4***we*/*our* birthdays aren't on the same day! **5***My*/*I* birthday is on 31st December, and **6***he*/*his* birthday is on 1st January.

b Complete the sentences using *Amy's*, *Fred's* or *Amy and Fred's*.

1 ___ birthday is on 31st December.
2 ___ birthday is on 1st January.
3 ___ birthdays aren't on the same day.

Everyday English

5 a Look at the timetable. Complete the questions.

— Timetable —

8.45	9.35	10.25		11.00	11.50	12.30
44 + 2 = 89 20 + 44 = 44			BREAK			

1 What time is **History**?
  It's at ten to twelve.
2 What time is ___ ?
  It's at half past twelve.
3 What time is ___ ?
  It's at twenty-five past ten.

b Look at the timetable. Write questions and answers about the other three subjects.

c Write three questions and answers about your lessons.

▶ **Workbook** pages 10–11, exercises 1–9

YOU FIRST! Are your feelings different at different times of the day?

My day, my feelings

1 It's seven o'clock. I'm sleepy.

a It's half past eleven. I'm thirsty. I'm in PE. It's my favourite subject.

b I'm tired. I'm on the school bus. It's ten past two.

2

c I'm bored. It's half past five. I'm with my mother in the supermarket. I don't like the supermarket!

6 ___

5 It's half past three. I'm in Drama club. I'm excited.

4 ___

3 It's quarter to one. I'm in Maths class. I'm hungry.

---

1 Look at Maria's project. Answer the questions.
1 She's sleepy. What time is it?
  It's seven o'clock.
2 She's hungry. Where is she?
3 She's tired. What time is it?

2 Read the sticky notes from Maria's project. Match the notes on the right (a–c) to the gaps (2, 4 and 6) in the picture. Complete the notes.

3 Look at Maria's project and the notes again. Answer the questions.
1 What colour is the picture for *sleepy*?
2 What colour is the picture for *thirsty*?
3 What colour is the picture for *hungry*?
4 Which feeling is grey in Maria's project?
5 Which feeling is orange in Maria's project?
6 Which feeling is white in Maria's project?
7 Do you like these colours for these feelings?

4 Create your own 'feelings wheel'. Follow the instructions. Ask your teacher for more information.
1 Think of four or five times in the day when you have different feelings.
2 Write two or three sentences about each time. Check them carefully.
3 Draw your 'feelings wheel'.
4 Draw a picture in each section. Choose a colour to represent the emotion.
5 Write your sentences on sticky notes. Stick them on your project.

5 Present your 'feelings wheel' to the class. Tell your friends about some of the things on your wheel. Answer their questions.

It's half past seven. I'm in bed. I'm hungry!

Which emotion is blue for you?

1 Culture

 YOU FIRST! Which countries speak English as a first language?

Do you speak English?

English is the first language in these countries. Some of the people in these countries speak two languages. In the USA, a lot of people speak Spanish. In Canada, a lot of people speak French. The Irish, the Welsh and the Scots speak English, and they speak their national languages, too.

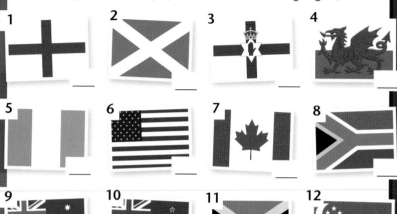

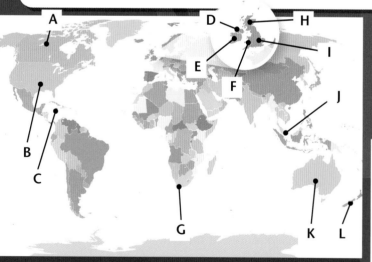

The countries of England, Northern Ireland, Scotland and Wales make the United Kingdom. This is the United Kingdom flag. It is made of the Northern Irish, Scottish and English flags.

a The Irish flag is green, white and orange.

b The Scottish flag is blue, with a white cross on it.

c The English flag is white, with a red cross on it.

d The Welsh flag is green and white, with a red dragon on it.

e The Jamaican flag is green and black, with a yellow cross.

f The Australian flag is red, white and blue, with six white stars.

g The Canadian flag is red and white, with a leaf on it.

h The American flag is red, white and blue, with 50 stars on it.

i The Northern Irish flag is white, with a red cross and a star on it.

j The New Zealand flag is red, white and blue, with four red and white stars.

k The South African flag is red, black, blue, green, white and yellow.

l The Singaporean flag is red and white, with five white stars and a white moon.

Glossary

cross   dragon   star   leaf   moon

3 ◀) **1.35** Listen and complete the chart with **T** (true) or **F** (false). Correct the false sentences.

	I'm from the UK.	I can speak English and another language.
David	T	
Celine		
Carol		
Lorcan		

1 Read the introduction and descriptions (a–l). Label the flags (1–12).

2 a Get ready to speak Find the countries in exercise 1 on the map.

b Work with a partner. Ask and answer.

What's this country?   It's the USA.

Study tip!

The **Culture** pages give you a window into English-speaking countries. Compare them with your culture.

▶ Video My day

Learn through English

YOU FIRST! What different ways can you tell the time?

Sundials

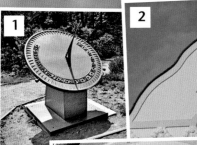
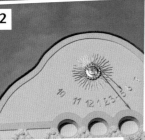

shadow

These are sundials.

You can tell the time with a sundial.

Some sundials are 1,500 years old.

a You can see sundials in cities.

b You can make a sundial. It's easy!

c You can find sundials in parks.

d You can be part of a sundial.

e You can see sundials on houses.

1 **a** Look at the photos. How many sundials can you see?

b Read the descriptions. Match the sentences (a–e) to the pictures (1–5).

Make a sundial

a You need: a stick, stones, chalk, a watch, a bucket

b You can make your sundial in the garden. Put the stick in the bucket.

c It's seven o'clock in the morning. Mark the shadow of the stick with a stone. Write '7' on the stone. Don't move the bucket!

d It's eight o'clock in the morning. Mark the shadow of the stick with a stone. Write '8' on the stone.

e Mark the shadow of the stick every hour. Stop at night. Your sundial is finished!

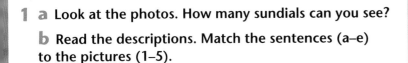

stick   stones   chalk   watch   bucket

2 Look at the pictures. Match the instructions to the pictures.

3 Over to you! Work with a partner. Ask the time in the different sundials on this page.

What time is it on this sundial?   It's four o'clock.

At home

2A My room

YOU FIRST! What colours can you see in your room?

Vocabulary

1 a Complete the labels with the words in the box.

laptop   poster   TV

1 ___

2 ___

3 wardrobe

5 rug

4 floor

A

6 door

7 lamp

8 shelf/shelves

9 window

10 ___

11 chair

12 bed

14 plant

13 box

15 desk

B

b 🔊 **1.37** Listen and check, then repeat.

Look!

Regular plurals	Irregular plural
bed → beds	shelf → shelves
wardrobe → wardrobes	
box → boxes	

2 a Read and complete the dialogue with a word from exercise 1a.

It's white.

Is it the ____ in picture A?

No, it isn't.

Is it the box in picture B?

Yes, it is.

b 🔊 **1.38** Listen and check, then repeat.

c Play the *Guess the Picture* game. Change the highlighted words in the dialogue.

▶ **Workbook** page 12, exercises 1–2

Grammar *have got; a, some, any*

3 a 🔊 **1.39** **Read and listen to the dialogue. Which picture in exercise 1 is Ug's room?**

Fred Tell me about your new room, Ug.

Ug I've got a bed and I've got some chairs.

Fred Have you got a door?

Ug No, I haven't. I haven't got a door and I haven't got any windows. It's very cold!

Fred Have you got any rugs?

Ug Yes, I have. I've got two, a tiger rug and a bear rug. Listen.

Fred Oh! That's nice!

b **Look at the dialogue. Match the sentence halves.**

1 I've got	**a** a bed.
2 I haven't got	**b** **any** windows.
3 I've got	**c** a door.
4 I haven't got	**d** **some** chairs.

> We use *have got* to talk about our possessions. Use *have got* with *I, you, we,* and *they.*

➕	➖
I've got	I haven't got
you've got	you haven't got
we've got	we haven't got

I've got = I have got

c **Look at Ug's room in exercise 1a. Are the sentences true (T) or false (F) for Ug?**

1 I've got a lamp. F
2 I haven't got a TV.
3 I've got some plants.
4 I haven't got any boxes.
5 I've got a laptop.

4 **Work with a partner. Answer Chris's question.**

> Which words change places in the question?

> You've got a chair in your room.
> Have you got a chair in your room?

5 a **Look at the dialogue in exercise 3b again. Find examples of *a/an*, *some* and *any*. When do we use them? Copy and complete the table.**

	About one thing	About more than one thing
➕	a table	___ plants
➖	___ bed	any books
❓	___ desk	___ shelves

b **Complete the sentences with *a, some,* or *any.***

1 I've got a TV in my room.
2 I haven't got ___ plants in my room.
3 I've got ___ shelves.
4 I haven't got ___ rug in my room.

c **Complete the questions with *a* or *any*. Then answer the questions for you.**

1 Have you got ___ desk in your room?
2 Have you got ___ rugs in your room?

> You can answer like this:
> Yes, I have.   No, I haven't.

Study tip!

Compare English to your language. Make a note of things which are similar and things which are different. Translation is not always a good idea!

➤ **Workbook** page 13, exercises 3–5

Speaking

6 a **Get ready to speak** **Look at Ug's room in exercise 1a again. What are Ug's answers to the questions?**

1 Have you got any plants in your room?
2 What colour are they?
3 Have you got a poster in your room?
4 What colour is it?

b 🔊 **1.40** **Listen and check.**

7 a **Make a list of five things in your room.**

e.g.: a blue bed, a red rug...

b **Work with a partner. Ask your partner about their room. Use the questions and answers in exercise 6a. Change the highlighted words.**

EXTRA Write three important things to remember from this lesson.

2B My pets

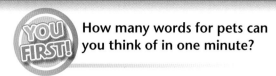

YOU FIRST! How many words for pets can you think of in one minute?

Vocabulary

1 a Complete the labels with the words in the box.

> cat   dog   hamster   iguana   mouse

9 parrot

10 monkey

11 canary

4 ___

12 goldfish

8 rabbit

13 ___

1 ___

2 frog

5 ___

6 guinea pig

14 turtle

7 snake

Look!
one mouse → two ~~mouses~~ mice
one foot → two ~~foots~~ feet

b 🔊 **1.41** Listen and check, then repeat.

2 a 🔊 **1.42** Listen and repeat.

> Have you got a parrot?
>
> No, I haven't.
>
> Me neither.
>
> Have you got a hamster?
>
> Yes, I have.
>
> Oh! I haven't.

b Imagine you have got three pets. Write them on a piece of paper. Ask your classmates about their pets. Can you find someone with the same pets as you on their list?

c Ask your friends about their real pets and answer their questions.

Vocabulary and Listening

3 🔊 **1.43** Listen and repeat the body parts.

a
1 body
2 wings
3 foot/feet
LOST! Call: 01632 960885

b
4 head
5 eyes
LOST! Call: 01632 960885

c
6 nose
7 mouth
LOST! Call: 01632 960885

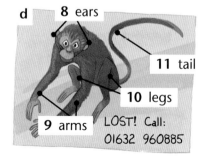

d
8 ears
9 arms
10 legs
11 tail
LOST! Call: 01632 960885

4 🔊 **1.44** Listen to the dialogues. Which animal are they talking about?

1 ___   2 ___   3 ___   4 ___

▶ **Workbook** page 14, exercises 1–2

Grammar *have got/has got*

5 a Match the animals to the descriptions.

> frog   monkey   parrot   snake

1 It's got long arms and legs.
2 It hasn't got a tail.
3 Has it got wings? Yes, it has.
4 Has it got legs? No, it hasn't.

> We use **have got** with **I, you, we** and **they.**

> We use **has got** with **he, she** and **it.**

> It's got long arms. =
> It has got long arms.
> It's brown. = It is brown.

b Complete the sentences with the correct form in the box.

> hasn't got   haven't got   has got   've got

1 I ⊕ ___ a rabbit.
2 My friend ⊕ ___ a canary.
3 I ⊖ ___ a dog.
4 My grandma ⊖ ___ a cat.

6 a Make sentences about the mouse in exercise 1. Use the words in the box.

> ~~a long tail~~   arms   big ears
> four legs   green eyes   wings

It's got a long tail.

b Answer the questions for the goldfish. Use *Yes, it has* or *No, it hasn't.*

1 Has it got eyes?   4 Has it got a tail?
2 Has it got wings?   5 Has it got arms?
3 Has it got ears?

▶ **Workbook** pages 14–15, exercises 3–6

Speaking

7 a Get ready to speak **Complete the dialogue with an animal from exercise 1.**

A Guess my animal.   B Is it yellow?
B Has it got four legs?   A Yes, it is.
A No, it hasn't.   B Is it a ___ ?
B Has it got wings?   A Yes, it is. Now it's
A Yes, it has.   your turn.

b 🔊 **1.45** Listen and check.

8 Work with a partner. Play the *Guess the Animal* game. Student **A** thinks of an animal. Student **B** asks questions and guesses the animal. Then swap.

Writing

9 Get ready to write **Look at the poster and read the advert for a lost cat. Complete the gaps.**

LOST!

This is Samson. He's my ¹___ . He's black and ²___ . He's got big ears and green ³___ . He's got a short tail and his ⁴___ are white.

Please help me find Samson.
Call 0117 49638101

> **Look!**
> We use adjectives like this.
> His eyes are **pink**.   He's got a **pink** nose.

▶ **Workbook** page 15, exercises 7–8

10 Write an advert for a lost pet.

1 Make a concept map and complete it for your pet.
2 Write your advert in rough.
3 Check your advert carefully. Check the verbs. Check the word order.
4 Write your advert in neat. You can draw a picture, too.

> **Study tip!**
> Concept maps help you organize information. You can use them with vocabulary and grammar, too.

 Make a wordsnake with words from this lesson. Can you make a snake with ten words?

goldfish – head – dog...

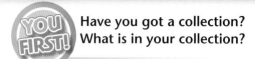

Have you got a collection?
What is in your collection?

1 a 🔊 **1.46** ▶ Read and listen to the story.
What can't Finn find?

b **Read the story again. Match the sentence halves.**

1 They look for Chris in   a in the dinosaur collection.

2 Lily can't see Chris   b it's Chamelemon.

3 Lily can see a chameleon   c Finn's room.

4 It isn't Chris;   d in Finn's superhero figures.

5 Chris can see a fly   e in the box.

6 Chris has got a key ring   f in her mouth.

Vocabulary

2 a Complete the labels with the words in the box.

dinoaur football card
magnet superhero figure

sticker ___

fossil ___ comic magazine

badge key ring ___ ___

b 🔊 **1.47 Listen and check, then repeat.**

**3 a Find the things from exercise 2 in the story,
then read and complete the dialogue.**

A They start with 'm'.
B Are they in the living room?

A Yes, they are.
B I know: ___ !

b 🔊 **1.48 Listen and check.**

**4 Over to you! Work with a partner. Play the *Guessing
game*. Use the dialogue in exercise 3 to help you.**

Look!

Chris is **in** the box. Sid is **on** the shelf.

➤ **Workbook** page 16, exercises 1–3

Pronunciation /ɒ/ /ɔː/

5 🔊 **1.49 Listen and repeat.**

Who's got my fossils?	Look in your boxes.
Where's my blue ball?	Look on the door.
Who's got my comics?	Look in the wardrobe.
Where's my dinosaur?	Oh, they're here!
	On the floor!

➤ **Workbook** page 16, exercise 4

Grammar Question words

**6 a Look at the story and find the questions.
Complete the questions with *How many* or
*What.***

1 ___ figures have you got?
2 ___ have you got in the box?

**b Find the answers to the questions in
the story.**

We use **What** to ask about **things**.

We use **How many** to ask
about **numbers of things**.

c Order the words to make questions.

1 has What on the shelf got Finn
in his bedroom ?
What has Finn got on the shelf in his bedroom?
2 Lily got What on her school bag has ?
3 Finn key rings got has How many ?
4 How many has fossils got Finn ?

**d Look at the pictures in the story and
answer the questions for Finn and Lily.**

He's got some dinosaurs and some comics.

➤ **Workbook** pages 16–17, exercises 5–6

Speaking

7 Get ready to speak Follow the instructions.

1 Draw two boxes.
Use different colours.
Imagine four collections.
Write the name of the
collections and the number
of items on the boxes.

6 football cards
8 fossils

2 Now draw two more
boxes. Don't write on
these pictures.

14 stickers
27 magnets

**8 Work with a partner. Ask and answer and
complete your empty pictures with your
partner's information.**

➤ **Workbook** page 17, exercise 7

**EXTRA How many words can you write that
begin with these letters?**

ON MY SHELF

O = orange, one,...

What can you remember about the children in the story?

Vocabulary

1 🔊 **1.50** Listen and repeat the rooms.

▶ **Workbook** page 18, exercise 1

2 a 🔊 **1.51** ▶ Read and listen to the story. What is in the bedroom, the living room and the kitchen?

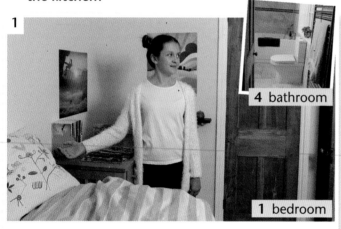

4 bathroom

1 bedroom

Rosie	This is the bathroom, and this is my bedroom.
Leila	It's great!
Jan	Hey! Are those Megaman comics?
Rosie	Yes, they are.
Jan	I love Megaman! Can I borrow a comic?
Rosie	Yes, of course.

3 living room

Rosie	This is the living room.
Jan	Hi Joel! Wow! These are brilliant video games.
Rosie	My dad collects video games. He's got hundreds.
Jan	Look! He's got my favourite game! Can I take a video game home, please?
Rosie	Sorry, you can't. I can't touch my dad's things.
Joel	Come and play with me.

2 garden

Leila	The boys aren't fun.
Rosie	They're boring.
Leila	Hey! Is that chocolate cake?
Rosie	Yes, it is. Mum's chocolate cake is amazing!
Leila	I'm hungry. Can I have some cake, please?
Rosie	Mum! Where are you?
Mum	I'm in the kitchen.
Rosie	Can we have some cake, please?
Mum	OK. But don't eat it all!

4 Later

5 kitchen

Jan	Where are Rosie and Leila?
Joel	I don't know.
Jan	Rosie! Leila! Where are you?
Rosie	We're in the kitchen.
Mum	Hi boys. Do you like chocolate cake?
Jan + Joel	Yes, we do!
Mum	Hey! Where's the cake?
Rosie + Leila	Too late!

b Read again. Answer the questions.

1 What has Rosie got in her bedroom?
2 Where are Rosie's dad's video games?
3 Where's Rosie's mum?
4 Can Jan and Joel see the cake?

Grammar *this, that, these, those*

3 a Match the sentence halves. You can find the sentences in the story.

1 This *is*	a Megaman comics?
2 *Are* those	b my bedroom.
3 These *are*	c a chocolate cake?
4 *Is* that	d brilliant video games.

This is my cake!

These are my games.

That is your cake!

Those are your games.

We use **this** and **these** to talk about things that are near.

We use **that** and **those** to talk about things that aren't near.

b Copy and complete the table with *this, that, these* and *those*.

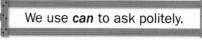

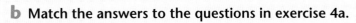

	this	

> **Workbook** page 18, exercise 2

Everyday English

4 a Who asks these questions in the story?

1 Can I borrow a comic?
2 Can I take a video game home, please?
3 Can we have some cake, please?

We use **can** to ask politely.

Don't forget to say 'please'!

b Match the answers to the questions in exercise 4a.

a Sorry, you can't. **b** OK. **c** Yes, of course.

c 🔊 **1.52** Listen and check, then repeat.

d How do you ask permission politely in the situations?

1 You haven't got a pencil. Ask your friend for his pencil. *Can I borrow a pencil?*
2 You are hungry. Ask your friend's mum for a biscuit.
3 You are thirsty. Ask your friend's dad for some water.
4 You haven't got your English book. Ask your friend for their book.
5 You're cold. Ask your friend for a hat.

> **Workbook** page 18, exercise 3

Listening and Speaking

Study tip!

Pictures give you a lot of information when you listen to English. Look at them carefully and think of the words in the pictures.

5 a Look at the pictures. What can you see? Match the places (1–4) to the things (a–d).

1    2

3    4

a    b

c 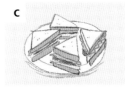   d

b 🔊 **1.53** Listen to the dialogues and check.

6 a 🔊 **1.54** Get ready to speak Listen to the first dialogue again and complete the sentences.

A This is the ___ .
B Are those Animal World ___ ?
A Yes, they are.
B Can I borrow a ___ , please?
A Yes, ___ .

b 🔊 **1.54** Listen again and repeat.

7 a Work with a partner. Choose another picture from exercise 5a. Make the dialogue for it.

b Act out your dialogue for the class. Can they guess which picture it is?

 EXTRA How can you explain the words *this, that, these* and *those* to a friend without translating?

Story

Read the story on page 19 of the Workbook and do the exercises.

Vocabulary and Grammar

1 a Label the picture.

1 ___
2 ___
5 ___
4 ___
3 ___
6 ___
10 ___
9 ___
8 ___
7 ___
11 ___
12 ___
14 ___
13 ___
15 magnet
16 ___

b Look at the picture and complete the sentences.

1 I've got seven ___ .
2 I've got nine ___ .
3 I've got four ___ .
4 I've got eight ___ .
5 I've got two ___ .

c Make three true sentences for you.

2 Look at the picture in exercise 1a and write questions and answers for the items in brackets.

1 (badges) Has he got any badges? Yes, he has. How many badges has he got? He's got nine.

2 (superhero figures) ___

3 (comics) ___

3 a Read the sentences and write the name of the animal.

1 It's got two legs and two wings. It hasn't got a nose. It's red, blue and green. ___

2 It hasn't got legs, arms or ears. ___

3 It's got long ears and a small tail. ___

4 It's green and it's got a big mouth. ___

b ✍ Write a description of one animal. Swap with a partner and guess their animal.

4 Write the names of places at home that begin with these letters.

1 l___ ___   2 k___   3 be___   4 g___   5 ba___

5 Make sentences with *this, that, these* or *those*.

1 This is my rabbit.

2 ___

3 ___   4 ___

Everyday English

6 Complete the sentences with the words in the box.

> borrow   ~~Can~~   Can   course   please   sorry

A <u>Can</u> I ___ your pencil, ___?

B Yes, of ___.

A ___ I take a video game home?

B No, ___, you can't.

▶ **Workbook** pages 20–21, exercises 1–6

YOU FIRST! Imagine a fantastic bedroom for you. What's in it?

My BRILLIANT bedroom

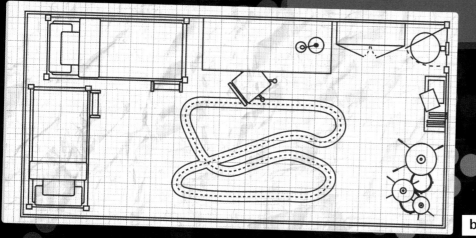

This is my brilliant bedroom. It's got four beds. They are for me and my three best friends.

b

c

a

1 I love basketball. I've got a basketball hoop near the door. I'm in the school team.

2 These are my shelves. My comic collection is on the shelves. My school books are on the shelves, too. I've got a desk and a lamp in my room, too.

d

3 This is my key ring collection. I've got 16 key rings!

4 This is my blackboard wall. I can draw and write on the wall. I've got a poster on the wall, too.

4 Now create your own brilliant bedroom. Follow your teacher's instructions.

1 Makes notes about your brilliant bedroom.
2 Draw a plan of your room or make a plan of your room with an app.
3 Make a 3-D view of your room.
4 Write two or three sticky notes to explain some of the things in the room. Check the sticky notes carefully for spelling and grammar.

1 Look at Steve's project. What has he got in his brilliant bedroom?

2 🔊 **1.55** Read and listen to Steve's project. Match the notes (1–4) to the arrows (a–d).

3 Look at the picture and the notes again and answer the questions.

1 What are two unusual or interesting things in the room?
2 What can you discover about Steve from his picture?
3 Find two pieces of extra information about Steve in the notes.

5 a Present your bedroom to the class. Tell your friends about the important things in your room.

b Listen to your friends. Ask a question.

What have you got on the shelves?

Have you got a TV in your room?

Where can you see interesting collections in your area?

Collections

The Eden Project, Cornwall, UK

The Eden Project, Cornwall

The Eden Project has got an amazing collection of plants. The plants are from different parts of the world. It's got a collection of food plants, like coffee and tea. It's got a collection of useful plants, like bamboo. It's got a collection of exotic plants, too.

Titan Arum
2 m
flower
3 m

This plant is from the rainforests of Indonesia. The flower is very, very big. It is 2 metres tall and 3 metres across. The plant has a flower every nine years. It's a very special flower!

Pitcher plant
cup
insect

This plant is from Borneo and Sumatra. The plant has got special cups. Insects fall in the cups. Then the plant uses the insect body for food. It is a carnivorous plant.

The British Museum
London, UK

The British Museum has got a collection of things from different parts of the world: Greece, Egypt, Mexico, Italy, etc.

This is a famous Aztec snake from Mexico. It isn't real: it's got two heads! It is made of wood and blue, red, white and black stones. It's very beautiful. It's about 500 years old.

You can see pets, too. These are mummies of real cats. They are in the Ancient Egypt room. They are part of the mummy collection. They are about 2,000 years old.

1 What can you see in the photos?

2 a Choose *The Eden Project* or *The British Museum*. Read about it. Say 3–5 things you can see in their collection.

b Answer the questions about your text.

The Eden Project

1 What are the collections in the Eden Project?

2 Why is the Titan Arum special?

3 Where is the pitcher plant from?

4 Why is the pitcher plant special?

The British Museum

5 Where are the collections in the British Museum from?

6 How many heads has the Mexican snake got?

7 What is the Mexican snake made of?

8 How old is the cat mummy?

c Work with a partner. Tell your partner about your text.

3 Over to you! **Think about you and your country. Answer the questions.**

1 Which collection do you like on this page? Why?

2 What can you see in your favourite collection in your area?

 ▶ **Video** Two collections

YOU FIRST! Where can you see birds' homes?

Birds and their nests

Birds make a home, or nest, for their chicks. You can see four different nests in the photos.

a

hedge

grass

b

hole

c

d

chicks

roof

mud

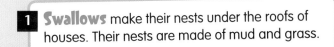
stones

1 **Swallows** make their nests under the roofs of houses. Their nests are made of mud and grass.

3 **Penguins** can't fly. They can't make their nests in trees. They make their nests on the ground. They use stones.

2 **Owls** make their nests in holes in trees. Their chicks are safe in the hole.

4 **Sparrows** make their nests in hedges or in the walls of houses. Their nests are made of grass, feathers, and hair.

1 Read the introduction. Are all nests the same?

2 Read about the nests and match the texts (1–4) to the photos (a–d).

3 Read the texts again and answer the questions for each bird.

4 Over to you! Find photos of birds' nests. Tell your partner about them.

> This is a swallow's nest. We've got swallows' nests in our garden...

	Sparrow	Owl	Penguin	Swallow
1 Where can you see this bird's nest?				
2 What is its nest made of?				
3 How many chicks can you see in the photo?				

1 🔊 **1.56** ▶ Read and listen to the story.

3 My day, your day

3A Different days, different routines

Is your routine the same every day?

Vocabulary

1 a Complete the labels with the words in the box.

> do my homework   get the bus
> go to school   have lunch   wash my hands

1 get up

2 get dressed

3 _____

4 wash my face

5 _____

6 have a shower

7 have breakfast

8 _____

9 have a snack

10 have dinner

11 _____

12 go to bed

13 go home

14 brush my teeth

15 _____

b 2.02 Listen and check, then repeat.

Study tip!

Organizing words in groups makes them easy to remember. You can write the groups in different colours, or put them in different shapes in your vocabulary book.

2 Over to you! Work with a partner. Tell your partner about your routine. Are your routines the same?

> I get up, then I have a shower. What about you?

> I get up, then I have breakfast.

> **Workbook** page 24, exercises 1–3

Listening and Grammar

Present simple: *I, you, we, they*

3 a Look at the photos. Match the words to photo A or photo B.

> get the bus   make lunch
> go to school   learn in the forest

A

B

b 🔊 **2.03** Listen to Amy and Tom. Which photo are they in?

c Who says the sentences, Tom, Amy or Grandma?

1 When do you have Forest School?
2 We don't get the bus.
3 Do you like Forest School?
4 We don't do homework on Fridays.
5 What time do you get up?
6 I get up at half past seven.
7 I get the bus.

d 🔊 **2.03** Listen again and check.

> These sentences are in the **present simple**.
> We use the present simple to talk about our routines.

4 a Complete the table with *do* or *don't*.

Present simple	
➕	I get the bus.
➖	I ___ get the bus.
❓	___ you get the bus? Yes, I ___ . No, I ___ .
❓	What time ___ you get the bus?

> You can use this table to help you make sentences in the present simple.

b Match the sentence halves.

1 We use **do**
2 We use **don't**

a to make negative sentences and in short answers.
b to make questions and in short answers.

5 a Complete the sentences for Amy.

> don't do   don't get
> ~~don't go~~   like   make   walk

1 I don't go to school on Fridays.
2 I ___ the bus.
3 We ___ to the forest.
4 We ___ our lunch on a fire.
5 I ___ Fridays.
6 I ___ homework on Fridays.

b 🔊 **2.04** Listen and check.

c Put the words in the correct order to make questions for Tom.

1 get up   What time   you   do   ?
2 have breakfast   do   What time   you   ?
3 Do   to school   you   walk   ?
4 the bus   you   What time   do   get   ?
5 What time   start   do   classes   ?

d 🔊 **2.05** Listen again. Then answer the questions for Tom.

1 I get up at half past seven.

> ▶ **Workbook** page 25, exercises 4–6

Speaking

6 a Get ready to speak **Put the lines of the dialogue in the correct order.**

___ **What time do you go to bed?**
___ Yes, I do. I play basketball on Wednesdays, and I go to guitar class on Thursdays.
7 **When do you do your homework?**
1 **What time do you go home?**
___ I go home at half past three.
4 I have a snack, and then I watch television.
___ **Do you do any activities in the afternoon?**
___ Before dinner.
___ At about half past nine or ten.
___ **What do you do after school?**

b 🔊 **2.06** Listen and check.

Look!

| in the morning | in the afternoon | in the evening | at night |

c Answer the questions in exercise 6a for you.

7 Work with a partner. Ask and answer the questions in exercise 6a. Do you have anything in common?

 Make a zigzag book with seven pages and write the days of the week on them. Write one or two different sentences about your routine for every day.

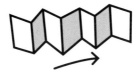

Do you celebrate Book Day? Who are your favourite fictional characters?

Vocabulary

1 a Match the pictures to the words in the box.

> do karate   drive a car   go to the library
> live in London   read books   ride a bike
> ride a horse   watch TV   work

b 🔊 2.07 Listen and check, then repeat.

2 a Look at the picture and complete the dialogue.

> Is it 'do karate'?

> No, it isn't! Try again.

> I know! It's '___'!

> That's right! It is.

b 🔊 2.08 Listen and check, then repeat.

c Work in small groups. Play the *Miming game*.

> **Workbook** page 26, exercises 1–2

Reading and Grammar

Present simple: *he/she/it*

3 Read about Alex Rider. Choose the correct picture.

a Alex Rider

b Alex Rider

c Alex Rider

BOOK DAY

☺ *Year 5's favourite books and characters*

I love the Alex Rider books by Anthony Horowitz. Alex Rider is my hero. He's 14 years old. He's got brown eyes and short brown hair. He's a student at Brookland Comprehensive School. He doesn't live with his parents; he lives in London with his guardian, Jack Starbright.

Alex doesn't go to school every day. He's a spy; he works for MI6. He doesn't drive a James Bond car, but he rides an amazing bike with lots of spy gadgets. He speaks four languages. He likes sport. He plays football and he does karate. He's a black belt. Alex's surname is Rider, but does he like horses? No, he doesn't! Alex has fantastic adventures in the books. I recommend them!

4 a Read the text again. Match the sentence halves.

1 Alex **lives**   a horses?
2 Alex **doesn't go**   b four languages.
3 Alex **speaks**   c in London.
4 **Does** he like   d to school every day.

> These sentences are in the **present simple**, too.

> Be careful! The verb changes in *he*, *she*, *it* sentences.

I live…	→ He lives…
I don't drive…	→ She **doesn't drive**…
Do you speak…?	→ **Does** she **speak**…?

b Match the sentence halves to make the rules.

1 We use *does*   **a** in negative sentences.
2 We use *doesn't*   **b** in positive sentences.
3 We add an *s* to   **c** to make questions.
the verb

> You can use the sentences in exercise 4a to help you make sentences about the present simple.

Remember!

I **have** lunch at two o'clock.
He **has** lunch at one o'clock.
NOT ~~He haves lunch at one o'clock.~~

c Answer the questions about Alex Rider.
Then write four more questions. Ask your partner.

1 Does he live with his mum and dad?
2 Does he live in London?
3 Where does he go to school?

d Complete the text about *Matilda* with the correct form of the verbs in the box.

> go   ~~live~~   read   read   watch

Remember!

She **lives** in London. She **doesn't live** in Leeds.

BOOK DAY

☺ *Year 5's favourite books and characters*

Matilda by Roald Dahl is my favourite book. Matilda is the main character. She ¹ ✓ *lives* with her parents and her brother, Michael. Michael ² ✗ ___ books; he ³ ✓ ___ television all day.

Matilda is clever. She loves books, and she ⁴ ✓ ___ to the library every day. The librarian is surprised! She ⁵ ✓ ___ books for children and books for adults, too. Her mum and dad don't understand Matilda. She isn't happy at home...

---

5 Over to you! Talk to your classmates about your favourite books or film characters.

> **Workbook** pages 26–27, exercises 3–5

Writing

6 Get ready to write Look at the notes about Alex Rider. Are they correct? Correct the incorrect information.

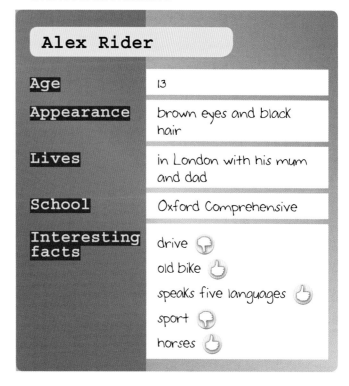

Alex Rider	
Age	13
Appearance	brown eyes and black hair
Lives	in London with his mum and dad
School	Oxford Comprehensive
Interesting facts	drive 👎
	old bike 👍
	speaks five languages 👍
	sport 👎
	horses 👍

> **Workbook** page 27, exercises 6–7

7 Write about a character in a book or film.

1 Choose a character from a book or a film you like.
2 Make notes about the character. Use the table in exercise 6.
3 Write your text in rough. You can use the texts about Alex or Matilda to help you.
4 Check your text carefully. Check the verbs are in the correct form.
5 Write your text in neat. You can add a picture, too.

Study tip!

Make a list of your common mistakes. Use it to help you check your writing.

What's your favourite book at the moment? Write three or four sentences about it.

YOU FIRST! What can you put in a sandwich?

1 a 🔊 **2.09** ▶ Read and listen to the story. Where is the chicken leg?

b Read the story again. Answer the questions.

1 Does Finn like eggs?
2 What kind of sandwiches does Dad like?
3 What does Sid want?
4 What is in Sid?
5 Where is Chris?

Vocabulary

2 a Look at the first picture in the story. Number the words in the box.

☐ banana	☐ brown bread	☐ butter
☐ cheese	☐ chicken	☐ egg	☐ ham	☐ jam
☐ salad	☐ salami	☐ tuna	☐ white bread

b 🔊 **2.10** Listen and check, then repeat.

▶ **Workbook** page 28, exercises 1–3

Pronunciation

3 🔊 **2.11** **Listen and repeat.**

Charles loves cheese and chocolate.
Jane loves orange jam.
I love tuna and chicken,
But I don't like bananas and ham!

▶ **Workbook** page 28, exercise 4

Grammar
Present simple: *love/like/don't like/hate*

4 a **Read the sentences in the table.
Which sentence is not in the story?**

	I, you, we, they	he, she, it
➕	I **hate** eggs.	She **loves** jam.
➖	I **don't like** brown bread.	He **doesn't like** cheese and ham.
❓	**Do you want** egg and cheese, too?	**Does Dad want** ham and cheese, too?
Wh- ❓	What **do you want** in your picnic?	What **does Sid want**?

b **Find two more present simple sentences in
the story and add them to the table.**

You can say what you **like** and
don't like with these words.

love   like   don't like   hate

c **Look at the table and complete the sentences
with the correct form of *love, like, don't like* or *hate*.**

	😋	👍	👎	😣
Zak	bananas	cheese	salami	eggs
Zoe	tuna	cheese	tuna	eggs

1 Zak *loves* bananas.
2 Zoe ___ tuna.
3 Zoe and Zak ___ eggs.
4 Zoe ___ cheese.
5 Zoe ___ chicken.
6 Zak ___ salami.

d **Complete the questions and answers about
Zak and Zoe.**

1 Does Zak like eggs?   No, he doesn't.
2 ___ Zoe like chicken?   ___
3 ___ Zak and Zoe like cheese?   ___
4 ___ Zak like salami?   ___

▶ **Workbook** page 29, exercises 5–7

Speaking

5 a Get ready to speak **Look at the pictures
and complete the dialogue.**

Do you want a ___ and ___ sandwich?

No, ___ , thank you.

Why not? It's delicious.

I ___ ___.

b 🔊 **2.12** **Listen and check, then repeat.**

6 a **Invent an amazing sandwich. Use the foods
in exercise 2.**

b **Work in groups. Offer your friends your
sandwich. Use the dialogue in exercise 5 to help
you. Can you find three people who want your
sandwich?**

EXTRA **Describe your perfect picnic. What is in
your picnic? Where is it? Who are you with?**

What food do you eat at parties?

1 a 🔊 **2.13** ▶ **Read and listen to the story. What does Aunt Edith eat?**

1

Mum Joel, Rosie! Are you ready for the party?

Rosie Yes, we are.

Mum Can you answer the door, please?

Rosie OK. Hello Aunt Edith. Come in.

Aunt Edith Thank you. I've got some cupcakes for the party.

Rosie Thanks. Come to the kitchen. You can give them to Mum.

2

Rosie Would you like a hot dog, Aunt Edith?

Aunt Edith No, thanks. I'm a vegetarian. I don't eat dogs.

Joel It isn't a dog! Oh, I see, that's a joke. Would you like a burger?

Aunt Edith No, thanks. Burgers are meat, too. I don't eat meat.

Joel Oh, yes. Of course. What would you like?

Aunt Edith I'd like a cheese sandwich, please.

Rosie OK. Wait a minute.

3

Rosie Sorry, we haven't got cheese sandwiches. But we've got pizza. It's cheese and tomato.

Aunt Edith Well, OK.

Joel Would you like some chilli sauce?

Aunt Edith I'm not sure.

Joel I love this chilli sauce. It's my favourite.

Aunt Edith Be careful!

Rosie Oh no! Don't eat that! The sauce is really, really hot.

4

Rosie Aunt Edith! Would you like a pie? They're vegetarian.

Aunt Edith Do they need chilli sauce?

Joel No, they don't.

Aunt Edith Good! Joel! Look out!

Rosie Oh no! The pies!

Aunt Edith Mine!

Rosie Well done, Aunt Edith! Finally you've got some food.

Aunt Edith Umm, thanks.

b Read again. Answer the questions.

1 What has Aunt Edith got for the party?

2 Does Aunt Edith eat meat?

3 Can Aunt Edith eat the pizza?

4 Does Aunt Edith save a hot dog?

Vocabulary

2 a Match the pictures (1–10) to the sentences (a–j).

a She hates **juice**.
b He likes **cupcakes**.
c He doesn't like **biscuits**.
d He loves **popcorn**.
e She doesn't like **apple pie**.
f He hates **crisps**.
g He likes **pizza**.
h She loves **hot dogs**.
i She doesn't like **burgers**.
j She likes **ice cream**.

b 🔊 **2.14** Listen and repeat the food words.

c Work with a partner. Which foods do you like?

▶ **Workbook** page 30, exercise 1

Everyday English

3 a Read the story again. Match the sentence halves.

1 Would you like
2 What would you
3 I'd like

a a cheese sandwich, please.
b a hot dog?
c like?

b Choose the correct answer for the sentences.

1 'Would you like a hot dog?' means…
  a Can you…?   b Do you want…?
2 'What would you like?' means…
  a What do you want?   b What have you got?
3 'I'd like a cheese sandwich, please' means…
  a I love…   b I want…

> You can answer polite questions like this.

Yes, please.   No, thanks.

c 🔊 **2.15** Listen and repeat the expressions.

d How can you say the questions politely?

1 What do you want for your snack today?
2 Do you want a cupcake?
3 Do you want some popcorn?
4 What do you want for dinner today?

e Over to you! Work with a partner. Ask the questions in exercise 3d and answer politely.

▶ **Workbook** page 30, exercises 2–3

Listening and Speaking

4 a Look at the pictures. Which words in the box do you think are in the dialogues?

> biscuit   burger   cheese   cupcake
> ice cream   juice   pizza   water

b 🔊 **2.16** Listen and check.

c Put the first dialogue in the correct order.

Boy	And I'd like an ice cream, too.	☐
Boy	Yes, please!	11
Mum	That's fine. I like cheese and ham, too.	☐
Boy	I'd like cheese and ham.	7
Mum	I'd like cheese and tuna.	☐
Mum	Would you like a pizza?	2
Boy	Oh, I don't like tuna.	5
Mum	Don't worry. What would you like?	☐
Mum	OK. Chocolate?	☐
Boy	Good idea. Yes, please.	☐
Boy	I'm hungry!	☐

d 🔊 **2.17** Listen again and check.

5 Get ready to speak Work in small groups. Prepare a menu. Use the words in exercise 2a.

6 Work with a partner. Decide what to order from your menu. Use the dialogue in exercise 4c to help you.

EXTRA Make four spidergrams for food. Use *I love, I like, I don't like* and *I hate*.

Story

Read the story on page 31 of the Workbook and do the exercises.

3 Revision

Vocabulary and Grammar

1 Answer the questions. Give more information for your *no* answers.

1 Do you get up at half past seven?

Yes, I do./No, I don't. I get up at quarter to eight.

2 Do you wash your hair every day? ___
3 Do you have breakfast at school? ___
4 Do you walk to school? ___
5 Do you have a snack in the morning? ___
6 Do you do your homework at three o'clock? ___

2 Look at the pictures. Make sentences about Sam.

Sam is my cousin. We are different.

me | Sam UNIVERSITY

1 Sam doesn't go to school. He goes to university.

2 ___

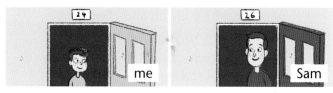

3 ___

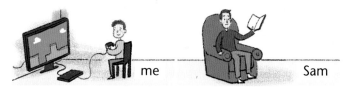

4 ___

5 ___

6 ___

3 a Write four sentences about Bea and Ben.

	Bea	Ben

1 (Ben/eggs) He hates eggs.
2 (Bea and Ben/tuna) They ___ .
3 (Bea/popcorn) She ___ .
4 (Ben/ice cream) He ___ .

b Write four questions and answers about Ben and Bea.

1 (Ben/eggs) Does he like eggs?

No, he doesn't.

2 (Bea and Ben/salad) ___ ? ___
3 (Ben/biscuits) ___ ? ___
4 (Bea/cupcakes) ___ ? ___

Everyday English

4 Match the questions (1–4) to the answers (a–d).

1 Would you like a sandwich?
2 Would you like some juice?
3 I'd like a cheese sandwich, please.
4 What would you like?

a I'd like a cheese and tuna pizza, please.
b Sorry, we haven't got any cheese.
c No, thank you. I'm not thirsty.
d Yes, please. I'm hungry.

▸ **Workbook** pages 32–33, exercises 1–7

YOU FIRST! What makes a great trip?

A great school trip

The Year 5 school trip

Year 5 goes on the same trip every year.
It's great!

09.30 They go to school in the morning, but they don't have classes. They get the bus at half past nine. They go to Oxford. It's a big city near their school.

10.30 They arrive in Oxford at half past ten. They visit the castle. Then they go on the ghost walk. The guide tells them about the ghosts in Oxford. It's scary!

1.00 They have a picnic lunch in a park. Every student takes a picnic. They take sandwiches, cakes, popcorn and fruit. They put the food on a big table and they share it. The food is delicious.

7.00 The bus leaves at six o'clock. They sing songs and play games in the bus. They arrive at school at 7.00. They're very tired.

3.30 They go to the Cotswold Wildlife Park. They have a snack in the café. They have a ride on the train in the park. They see rhinos and giraffes. Some years, the rhinos have babies. They're cute.

1.45 They go on a punt on the river. A punt is a kind of boat. It's long and thin. Every year a student falls in the river! It's very funny.

1 a Look at the photos in Mara's project. Choose the activities the Year 5 students do on their trip.

> climb a tree   go on the river   go to a museum
> have a picnic   see some animals   visit a castle

b Read Mara's project. Answer the questions.
1 What time do they leave school?
2 What does the guide do on the ghost walk?
3 Where do they have lunch?
4 Do all the students fall in the river?
5 What animals do they see?
6 What time do they leave Oxford?

2 Look at Mara's project again. Answer the questions.
1 What is the order of the boxes?
2 Can you find some opinions in Mara's project?
3 How does Mara use colours?

3 Now create your own great day out.
1 Where do you want to go on your trip? How?
2 Find information about things to do and see.
3 Decide on the schedule.
4 Find pictures to illustrate your project.
5 Write your texts. Check your spelling and grammar.

4 a Present your great school trip to the class.
b Listen to your friends. Ask a question.

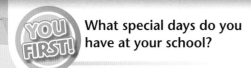

YOU FIRST! What special days do you have at your school?

SPECIAL days at SCHOOL

Sports Day at Hillside Primary

Our school is in Norwich, in England. We have Sports Day at school in June. It's a day for all the family. We have races for dads, mums, and teachers.

sack

We have traditional races on Sports Day. I love the sack race. You stand in a sack and you jump to the finishing line. It's very difficult! I like the egg and spoon race, too. The eggs fall off the spoons. Luckily the eggs are hard!

The School Fete at Little Hampton Primary School

Our school is in Melbourne, Australia. Our school fete is in November. It's a fantastic day. The school is open to family and friends. You can do great activities for one or two dollars. You can buy cakes, books, and toys, too. The school uses the money for books, computers, and sports equipment.

tractor

My friend Patrick's dad has got a tractor. It's very big. He gives tractor rides at the fete. It's brilliant! You can ride on ponies, too. My sister likes the pony rides. She loves horses!

1 Look at the photos. Match the sentences (a–d) to the photos (1–4).

  a This is the mums' race.

  b This is a photo of a sack race.

  c This photo is of a cake stall.

  d This photo is of the tractor rides.

2 Choose *Sports Day* or *The School Fete*. Read about them. Find three activities they do on these special days.

3 Work with a partner. Are the sentences about *Sports Day*, *The School Fete*, or both?

  1 You run races.

  2 You can buy cakes and books.

  3 You can ride on tractors and ponies.

  4 You have fun.

  5 All the family can go.

Glossary

spoon

hard

pony

4 ◀) **2.18** Listen to the announcements and match them to the photos.

5 Over to you! Work with a partner. Discuss your answers.

  1 Do you think Sports Day is fun? Why?

  2 Do you think The School Fete is fun? Why?

  3 What are traditional games in your country?

  4 How can you make money for your school?

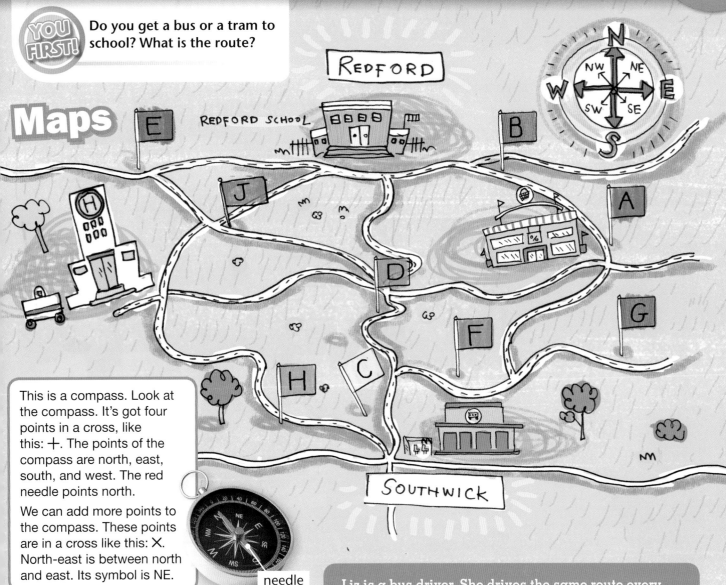

YOU FIRST! Do you get a bus or a tram to school? What is the route?

Maps

REDFORD

REDFORD SCHOOL

SOUTHWICK

This is a compass. Look at the compass. It's got four points in a cross, like this: +. The points of the compass are north, east, south, and west. The red needle points north.

We can add more points to the compass. These points are in a cross like this: X. North-east is between north and east. Its symbol is NE.

needle

Liz is a bus driver. She drives the same route every day. We can describe her route with compass points.

She starts at the bus station in Southwick. Then she drives **¹**north to bus stop D. She turns **²**___ and she stops at Megastore. Then she goes **³**___ to bus stop B. After bus stop B, she goes **⁴**___ and stops at Redford School. Then she goes **⁵**___ to bus stop J. After bus stop J, she stops at the hospital, and then she goes **⁶**___ to bus stop H. After bus stop H, she goes to the bus station again.

1 a Look at the compass and read the first paragraph. What do *N, W, E*, and *S* mean on the compass?

b Find the places on the map and complete the sentences.
1 Redford School is in the north.
2 Megastore is in the ___ .
3 The hospital is in the ___ .
4 The bus station is in the ___ .

c Read the second paragraph. What do *NE, SE, SW* and *NW* mean?

d Find the bus stops on the map. Answer the questions.
1 Is bus stop A in the north-west?
   No, it isn't. It's in the north-east.
2 Is bus stop H in the south-west? ___
3 Is bus stop G in the south-west? ___
4 Is bus stop J in the south-east? ___

2 Read the text and look at the map. Complete the bus driver's route with the points of the compass.

3 🔊 **2.19** Listen and follow Ivan's route on the same map. Write the names of the stops.

4 a Over to you! Invent a different route on the map.

b Work with a partner. Describe your route to your partner. Can he/she follow your route?

c Find or draw a map of your area. Describe how to go from your house to your school.

What do you do after school?

▶ **Workbook** page 34, exercise 1

Tilda

Nandi and Deela

Hilly

1 make her bed

Yip and Yap

2 dance

3 fly

Inga

Vorik

Jenna

Max

4 talk to

Zora and Felix

Zelda

Alf

5 cook

Jess

6 work

Rex

Tara

7 watch TV

Fento

Delta

Kitty

Tal

8 listen to music

Grammar Present continuous

1 a 🔊 **2.21** **Read and listen to the dialogues.**
Look at the picture. Who is Miss Cassie talking to
or about in each dialogue?

Miss Cassie	Come and have your snack.
1___	I can't! **I'm doing** my homework.
Miss Cassie	Go to the kitchen now, please. It's time for your snack.
2___ and **3**___	Not now, Miss Cassie! **We're playing** basketball.
Miss Cassie	Where's **4**___ ?
5___	**He isn't playing** with me. Oh no! I can see him now. **He's climbing** a rock!
Miss Cassie	**Are you having** your snack?
6___	Yes, I am. It's delicious!

Yuri

Arak

Goss

9 tidy up

What do the verbs
have in common?

The verbs are in the **present continuous**.

b Look at the sentences in exercise 1a again. Choose the correct answer to complete the rule.

We use the present continuous to…

a give instructions

b talk about now

c talk about routines

c Complete the sentences for Sid.

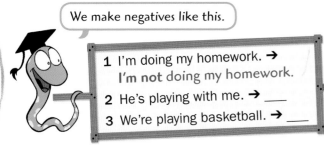

We make negatives like this.

1 I'm doing my homework. →
   I'm not doing my homework.

2 He's playing with me. → ___

3 We're playing basketball. → ___

d Now complete the sentence for Chris.

We make *yes/no* questions like this.

He **is** playing with me.
Is he playing with me?

Answer like this.

Yes, he is.
No, ___.

Look!

climb + -*ing* = climbing
write + -*ing* = writing
run + -*ing* = running

2 a Look at the picture in exercise 1. Are the sentences true (T) or false (F)? Correct the false sentences.

1 Inga is walking. F Inga isn't walking. She's running.

2 Max is writing. ___

3 Felix and Zora aren't riding their bikes. ___

4 Rex and Tara are playing football. ___

5 Tal is drawing. ___

b Are the sentences true for you? Correct the false sentences.

1 I'm playing in the playground.

   I'm not playing in the playground. I'm sitting in my classroom.

2 I'm doing my homework.

3 I'm studying Chinese now.

4 I'm writing.

▶ **Workbook** page 34, exercises 2–3

Vocabulary

3 a Look at the picture again. Complete the sentences with the correct name or names.

1 Felix is talking to Zora.

2 ___ is listening to music.

3 ___ is making her bed.

4 ___ are tidying up.

5 ___ is cooking.

6 ___ are flying.

7 ___ is sleeping.

8 ___ are dancing.

9 ___ is working.

b 🔊 **2.22** Listen and check, then repeat the verbs.

talk to   listen to   make her bed   tidy up
cook   fly   sleep   dance   work

c Work with a partner. Student **A** makes a sentence about someone in the picture in exercise 1. Student **B** says the name.

Who's this? She's running.

Inga.

That's right. Now it's your turn.

▶ **Workbook** page 35, exercises 4–5

Speaking

4 Get ready to speak   Work in teams of three or four. Write four sentences for the *Miming game*. Use the present continuous with *he, she,* and *they*.

5 Play the *Miming game*. Play against another team. Give one person (or two people) on the other team a sentence. Can he/she mime and the others guess your sentences?

Is she sleeping?

Yes, she is.

Are they making the beds?

No, they aren't.

EXTRA Imagine you aren't in English class. Where are you? Write five sentences.

   e.g.: I'm at home. I'm sleeping.

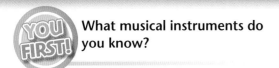 What musical instruments do you know?

1 a 🔊 **2.23** ▶ Read and listen to the story. Do they all like Finn's music?

b Read the story again. Answer the questions.

1 Is Finn doing English homework?

2 Is Finn writing some music?

3 Is Finn playing with a chicken?

4 Does Sid like Finn's composition?

5 Does Chris like Finn's composition?

6 Is Lily videoing Finn?

7 Is Lily dancing to the music?

Vocabulary

2 a Match the words in the box to the instruments (1–10) in the picture.

> bass guitar   cello   clarinet   drums   guitar   piano   recorder   saxophone   trumpet   violin

4 Nora + Hal
2 Joyce
3 Poppy + Lucas
6 Alice
7 Ruby
8 Mila
9 Gus + Maya
10 Jack
1 Emilia + Matt
5 Oscar

b 🔊 **2.24** Listen and check, then repeat.

Look!

I can play **the** piano.   I can't play **the** violin.

c Ask other students what instruments they can play. How many different instruments can your class play?

> Can you play the piano?

> Yes, I can. Can you?

> No, I can't.

➤ **Workbook** page 36, exercises 1–2

Pronunciation   /v/   /w/

3 🔊 **2.25** Listen and repeat.
Vera's playing the violin,
Wendy's watching TV,
Wilf is washing windows
On Wednesday at five past three.

➤ **Workbook** page 36, exercise 3

Grammar

Present continuous: *Wh-* questions

4 a Look at the story again. Match the questions to the answers.
1 What are you doing?
2 Where are you hiding?
3 Who are you videoing?

a I'm in the bathroom.
b Sid. Look at him!
c I'm writing some music for the concert.

b Look at the sentences in 4a. Complete the rules.
1 We use *What* to ask about ___ .
2 We use *Where* to ask about ___ .
3 We use *Who* to ask about ___ .

> a person
> a place
> an action

> We make **Wh-** questions like this.

> He's playing the recorder.
> What is he playing?
> They're playing the violin.
> What are they playing?

> We can ask general questions like this.

> What's Sid doing?

c Over to you! Work with a partner. Ask and answer questions about the cartoon stories in units 1, 2 and 3.

➤ **Workbook** page 37, exercises 4–6

Speaking

5 Get ready to speak Work in small groups. Think of a place and what you can do there. Create a frozen scene using some of the verbs.

6 Show your scene to the class. Ask them about your scene. Which team is the winner?

> What are we doing?

EXTRA Use your dictionary. Find the names of five more musical instruments in English.

4C At the park

 What can you do at your local park?

Vocabulary

1 a 🔊 **2.26** Listen and repeat.

A
1 kiss her mother
Rosa
Mum
2 give a present

B
3 eat a pie
Greg
Tiny

C
4 sit
Dad
Aunt Lexi

D
5 take a photo
Anna
Joe
6 stand

E
7 feed the ducks
Jenny

F
8 play chess
Ellie

G
Chris
9 drink a milkshake

b Look at the pictures and complete the dialogue.

What's the person doing?   She's ____ .

Is it Jenny?   That's right! Your turn.

c 🔊 **2.27** Listen and check.

d Over to you! Work with a partner. Ask and answer questions about the pictures.

▶ **Workbook** page 38, exercises 1–2

Reading and Grammar

Object pronouns

2 a Match the descriptions (a–g) to the pictures (A–G) in exercise 1a.

a You're in this photo! We can see your hands and legs, and we can see your milkshake.

b Ellie and I are playing chess. This is the chess champion Karla King. She's talking to us! I love Karla King. She's brilliant.

c This is my dad. He doesn't like the park. My Aunt Lexi is talking to him. Poor Dad!

d I'm Rosa and it's my birthday! Mum is giving me my present. It's a camera!

e These are some greedy ducks in the park. They are very hungry. My sister is feeding them. They are looking in my sister's bag.

f This is my brother, Greg. He's got a pie. He's eating it. The problem is Tiny the dog likes pies!

g These are my friends, Joe and Anna. Joe is taking a photo of Anna. Joe likes her. Anna likes my brother.

b Read the descriptions again. Answer the questions.

1 What's Mum giving Rosa?
2 What's Greg eating?
3 Does Tiny like pie?
4 Does Dad like the park?
5 Is Joe happy?
6 Are the ducks hungry?
7 Is Karla King playing chess?

The highlighted words are **object pronouns**.

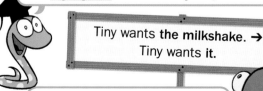

Tiny wants **the milkshake**. →
Tiny wants **it**.

We can use an object pronoun in the place of a person or a thing.

c Look at the sentences in exercise 2a again and complete the table.

Subject pronouns	Object pronouns
I	me
you	you
he	
she	
it	
we	
they	

Study tip!

Use the table to test yourself. Cover one column with a piece of paper, and write the words in the other column. Repeat until you have no mistakes.

d Change the **highlighted** words to the correct object pronoun.

1 She's scared of the ducks.
2 I'm really happy with my present.
3 He wants Greg's pie, too.
4 He doesn't like Aunt Lexi.
5 She's teaching me and my friend a new chess move.
6 Tiny is drinking your milkshake.
7 She's standing next to my brother.

e The sentences in exercise 2d are the last sentences of the descriptions in exercise 2a. Match the texts (a–g) to the sentences (1–7).

a–6

3 Change the **highlighted** words. You can find the answers in exercise 2.

1 He's eating it.
  He's eating a pie.
2 Aunt Lexi is talking to him.
  ____
3 Joe likes her.
  ____
4 My sister is feeding them.
  ____
5 She's talking to us.
  ____

▶ Workbook pages 38–39, exercises 3–4

Writing

4 Get ready to write Look at the picture and read the sentences. Write **D** (description) or **E** (extra information) next to each sentence.

1 We are in the park with our teacher. D
2 Our teacher's name is Miss Brown. ___
3 Miss Brown is taking a photo. ___
4 Anya and Katie are playing chess. ___
5 Anya is the chess champion of our school. ___
6 Pablo and Tina are feeding the ducks. ___
7 Tina loves animals. ___
8 Ahmed likes the park. ___
9 Sofia and Ahmed are sitting on the grass. ___

▶ Workbook page 39, exercise 5

5 Choose an interesting photo of your family or friends. Write about the photo.

1 Find and note the words you need.
2 Write about the photo. Include descriptions and extra information. Check your work carefully.

EXTRA Make a list of activities starting with the letters of your name. Then make a poem like this.

Sitting in my room
asking a question
reading a book
answering an email
having a cup of tea

Sarah is my name

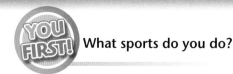
What sports do you do?

1 a 🔊 **2.28** ▶ **Read and listen to the story.**
What sports do they try at the leisure centre?

1

Jan I love sports! This is a great leisure centre.
Rosie Me too! What can we try today?
Leila Let's look at the noticeboard!
Rosie OK. We can play volleyball or go swimming.
Jan Let's try something new! Let's do athletics!
Rosie Great idea. Come on!

2

Joel I don't like athletics! It's difficult.
Rosie Me neither. I'm really tired.
Jan I'm not tired! I think athletics is fun.
Let's have a race.
Leila Oh no, not a race! No way!
Jan Don't be lazy! You can do it!
Rosie Come on. Let's try a different sport.
Leila Good idea. Fencing?
Joel OK. I'm sure fencing is easy.
Rosie Fingers crossed.

3

Jan What are you doing? Come and fight!
Leila I can't. My legs hurt.
Rosie Mine too!
Joel Fencing is difficult! I don't like it!
Jan Don't be silly! You can do it!
All No, we can't!
Jan Yes, you can! Try again.
Joel No way! Let's stop fencing. Let's climb the climbing wall.
Jan OK. Let's go!

4

Jan Hello down there! I'm at the top!
I'm the winner!
Leila This isn't fun.
Rosie My hands hurt.
Joel I'm hungry and thirsty.
Jan Hey, Leila, Joel! Help me climb down.
Leila Hmm. Sorry, but we're lazy and silly – we can't help you.
Rosie Hey! I've got a good idea. Let's go to the café.
Joel That's a great idea! Bye Jan!
Jan Help! Don't go!
Leila + Rosie Don't be silly! You can do it! Bye!

b Read the story again and answer the questions.
1 Is athletics a new sport for the children?
2 Do they all like athletics?
3 Do they all like fencing?
4 Do they help Jan climb down? Why?/Why not?

Vocabulary

2 a 🔊 **2.29** Listen and repeat.

Exeter Leisure Centre

Open Day! | **Try a new sport today!**

1 play badminton
2 play volleyball
3 do gymnastics
4 do athletics

5 do judo
6 go swimming
7 go fencing
8 go dancing

Look!
swim → go swimming   dance → go dancing

b Complete the dialogue.
A Do you play badminton?   B ✓ ___
A Do you do judo?   B ✗ ___

c Over to you! Ask your classmates about the sports they do. Can you find someone who does the same sports as you?

➤ **Workbook** page 40, exercises 1–2

Everyday English

3 a Look at the story. Who says the sentences?
1 Let's look at the noticeboard!
2 Let's do athletics!
3 Let's have a race.
4 Let's try a different sport.
5 Let's climb the climbing wall.
6 Let's go to the café.

We use *Let's* + **verb** to make a suggestion.

b Match the answers to the suggestions. Which are positive answers? Which are negative answers?
a That's a great idea!   d OK. Let's go!
b Good idea. Fencing?   e Great idea.
c OK.   f Oh no, not a race!

c 🔊 **2.30** Listen and check, then repeat.

d Practise the dialogues in pairs.

➤ **Workbook** page 40, exercises 3–4

Listening

4 a 🔊 **2.31** Which of the activities do you hear?

1
2
3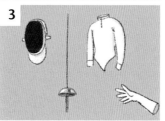
4
5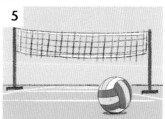
6
7

b 🔊 **2.31** Listen again and answer the questions for each dialogue.
1 What is the first idea?
2 Is there a second idea? If yes, what is it?
3 What do they do?

c 📝 Work with a partner. Can you remember one of the dialogues? Write it in your notebook. Then practise in pairs.

Speaking

5 Get ready to speak Imagine it is Saturday afternoon. You are with a friend. Think of three things you can do.

6 Talk to your classmates and suggest your ideas. Find someone who says yes to your ideas.

 EXTRA What are your top five activities for summer?

Story

Read the story on page 41 of the Workbook and do the exercises.

4 Revision

Vocabulary and Grammar

1 a Write one ➕ and one ➖ sentence about the people in the picture.

1 (sing) They aren't singing. They're dancing.
2 (read) ___
3 (watch TV) ___
4 (sleep) ___

b Write *yes/no* questions about the picture. Then write the answers.

1 (study) Is he studying? No, he isn't. He's tidying up.
2 (play video games) ___
3 (do homework) ___
4 (swim) ___

2 a Complete the sentences.

1 We're feeding the ducks.
2 ___ on a red chair.
3 ___ a milkshake.
4 ___ with her grandfather.
5 ___ to a woman.
6 ___ pies.
7 ___ the girl a sandwich.
8 ___ of our family.

b ✍ Rewrite the sentences. Replace the **highlighted** words with the correct object pronoun.

Everyday English

3 a Complete the chart with the sports.

play	1 b _ d _ _ n _ _ _ n
	2 v _ _ l _ y _ _ l _
do	3 g _ _ n _ _ t _ _ _ _
	4 a _ _ l _ _ i _ _
	5 j _ _ o
	6 f _ _ c _ _ g
go	7 s w _ _ m _ _ _ _
	8 d _ _ c _ _ _ _

b ✍ Write two mini-dialogues.

▶ **Workbook** pages 42–43, exercises 1–7

My after-school activities

Club Luna by Brad

I love After-School Club Luna. We do fun activities.

We are making moon cheese. We are using special moon milk. The cheese is delicious!

We're running and jumping at the Luna Sports Centre. Jumping is easy on the moon!

These are moon buggies. They are small cars. We're having a race! I'm in the red car. I'm winning!

Eco Club by Lily

I go to the Eco After-School Club on Fridays. We do lots of green activities.

We are making a solar oven from a pizza box. A solar oven cooks with the heat of the sun. It's amazing!

These are our seed bombs. They've got flower seeds in them. You can throw them on the ground and flowers grow.

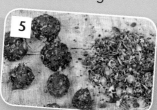

This is our photo safari. We are taking photos of the plants and animals in the park.

1 a Look at the two projects. Are they about real or imaginary after-school clubs?

b Match the titles (a–f) to the photos (1–6).

a Garden workshop
b Photo workshop
c Eco-tech workshop
d Driving workshop
e Cooking workshop
f Sports workshop

c Read the projects. Which club do you recommend for the students?

1 I want to drive a car.
2 I like technology projects.
3 I like cooking and I love cheese.
4 I think plants and flowers are very interesting.
5 I've got a new camera. I love it!
6 My favourite sport is athletics.

2 Look at the projects again. Copy and complete the concept map for one of the clubs.

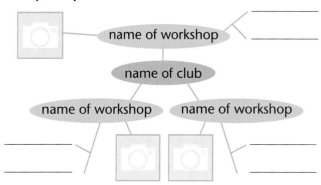

name of workshop

name of club

name of workshop   name of workshop

3 Now create your own after-school club poster.

1 Is your club real or imaginary?
2 Think about things to do at your club.
3 Make a concept map for your club.
4 Find pictures or photos for your album.
5 Write your texts. Check your spelling and grammar.

4 a Present your poster to the class. Tell your class about the photos.

b Listen to your classmates. Answer their questions.

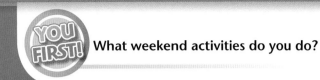 **What weekend activities do you do?**

Weekend fun

SCOTTISH DANCE SCHOOL

Do you like music? Do you like exercise? Come and learn Scottish country dances with us in the centre of Edinburgh!

Traditional Scottish country dances are fun. Some of the dances are very old, but people invent new dances every year. You dance in a group of 6–10 people. The dances are easy to learn. The music is fantastic. The musicians play traditional Scottish instruments like the bagpipes, the violin and the accordion.

About our classes

We've got classes for children and adults. We teach in schools, too. All our classes are in the afternoon.

We have a Ceilidh, or traditional Scottish dance, every Saturday afternoon. Come and join us!

For more information, call:
0131 496 4688

Surfing in Australia

Do you love the sea? Do you love sport? Come and learn to surf with us!

Surfing is a very popular sport in Australia. The weather is hot and sunny. We've got kilometres of beautiful beaches. Some beaches have small waves for learners. Some beaches have big waves for pros.

About our classes

We can teach you to bodyboard and to surf. Our Surf School is in Sydney, on the famous Palm Beach. We've got classes for adults and for children. We have small groups, and our teachers are very friendly!

For more information, call: 0491 570 158

Glossary

accordion   beach   wave   bodyboard

1 Look at the titles of the leaflets. Answer the questions.

1 What are the two texts about?

2 Which country are they in?

3 Which activity do you like?

2 a Choose a leaflet and read the information. Answer the questions about your text.

Scottish Dance School

1 Are all Scottish dances old?

2 Do you dance in pairs?

3 What do the musicians play?

Surfing in Australia

1 Do people like surfing in Australia?

2 Are all the beaches the same?

3 Where is the Surf School?

b Work with a partner. Ask and answer the questions, then give one more piece of information about your text.

3 a 🔊 2.32 Listen to the dialogue. Which school is he calling?

b 🔊 2.32 Listen again and answer the questions.

1 What does he want information about?

2 How old is his child?

3 When are the classes he chooses?

4 What's his child's name?

5 What can his child do?

4 Over to you! Work with a partner and answer the questions.

1 What weekend activities can you do in your country?

2 Are there traditional dances in your country?

3 What's a popular sport in your country?

▶ Video After-school clubs

Learn through English

 **Why do we have muscles?**

Muscles

Stretches

We use our muscles to move our bodies. We need healthy muscles. Healthy muscles are strong and flexible. Running, jumping and swimming make strong muscles. Stretching makes flexible muscles.

a She's sitting down. Her knees are bent. She's holding her feet.

b She's got her right arm in the air. She's touching her left foot with her left hand.

c He's standing up. His elbows are bent and his hands are behind his head.

e He's sitting down. His left foot is touching the top of his left leg. He's touching his right foot with his right hand.

d He's standing up, with his left leg in front of his right leg. His left knee is bent; his right leg is straight. His hands are on his left leg.

f She's standing on her left leg. She's holding her right foot with her right hand.

1 🔊 **2.33** **Listen and follow the instructions.**

2 **Read the introduction and answer the questions.**
1 What are healthy muscles?
2 What makes strong muscles?
3 What makes flexible muscles?
4 Are you using any muscles now? Where are they?

3 **Now read the second part of the article and match the descriptions of the stretches (a–f) to the pictures (1–6).**

4 **a** **Work with a partner. Ask and answer questions about the pictures. Use the phrases in the box.**

> ~~her back, arm and leg muscles~~
> his leg muscles   his leg and back muscles
> his arm and shoulder muscles
> her leg muscles

> Which child is stretching **her** back, arm and leg muscles?   It's number 1.

Glossary

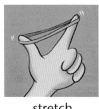

strong   flexible   stretch

b **Work with a partner. A does one of the stretches and B guesses the part of the body.**

> What am I stretching?   Your right leg.

5 **Over to you!** **Discuss the questions with a partner.**
1 Do you stretch before and after you do sport?
2 What stretches do you do?
3 Which muscles do they stretch?

1 🔊 2.34 ▶ Read and listen to the story.

5 In town

5A Our town

Vocabulary

1 a Complete the labels with the words in the box.

> café school supermarket swimming pool

1 shopping centre

2 ___

3 cinema

4 museum

5 ___

6 ___

7 hospital

8 ___

9 restaurant

10 library

b 🔊 **3.02** Listen and check, then repeat.

c 🔊 **3.03** Listen and repeat the dialogue.

A Is it a cinema?

B No, it isn't!

A I know! It's a hospital.

B That's right. Now it's your turn.

d Work with a partner. Play the *Draw and Guess* game.

➤ **Workbook** page 46, exercises 1–2

Pronunciation /θ/ /ð/

2 🔊 **3.04** Listen and repeat.

North, south, east, west,
This is the street I like best.
This is the cinema; that's my school.
This is the library, and that's the pool.
North, south, east, west,
This is the street I like best.

➤ **Workbook** page 46, exercise 3

Listening and Grammar

there is/there are

3 a 🔊 **3.05** Listen and match the dialogues to two of the street maps.

A

Mill Road

B

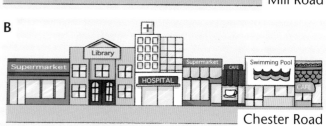
Chester Road

C

George Street

b 🔊 **3.05** Listen again and answer the questions for each dialogue.

1 Where is he/she now?

2 What is he/she doing?

3 What is his/her favourite place on the street?

4 a Look at the street maps again. Which map or maps are the sentences about?

1 Are there any restaurants? Yes, there are. A and C

2 There's a library.

3 There aren't any cafés.

4 There are two cinemas.

5 There's a museum.

6 Is there a swimming pool? Yes, there is.

7 There isn't a shopping centre.

b Match the sentence halves to complete the grammar rules.

1 We use **there is**

2 We use **there are**

a when we are talking about one thing.

b when we are talking about more than one thing.

c Look at the sentences in exercise 4a. Complete the table with the **highlighted** words.

	Singular	Plural
➕	There's	
➖		There aren't
❓	Is there...?	
Short answer		Yes, there are.
	No, there isn't.	No, there aren't.

We use *any* in ❓ and ➖.

Are there **any** cafés?
There aren't **any** supermarkets.

If we don't know the number, we can use *some*.

There are **two** restaurants.
There are **some** restaurants.

5 Complete the sentences about map A.

1 There's a school.

2 ___ any hotels.

3 ___ two restaurants.

4 ___ a library.

5 ___ a shopping centre.

6 a Over to you! Write some questions about maps A, B and C.

b Work with a partner. **A** chooses a map.
B asks questions about it and guesses the map.

Is there a swimming pool?

Yes, there is.

Are there any restaurants?

Yes, there are.

I know. It's map C.

▶ **Workbook** pages 46–47, exercises 4–5

Writing

7 Get ready to write Look at the maps in exercise 3.
Which street is the text about? Complete the text with the correct form of *there is/there are*.

This street is near my house. ¹There is a supermarket on the street. My dad works at the supermarket, and my mum works at the museum. ² ___ two restaurants, but ³ ___ a café. My school isn't on the street, but ⁴ ___ a bus stop. It's near the hospital. I get the bus at that stop. ⁵ ___ a swimming pool on the street, too. I love swimming, and I go to the pool on Fridays.

▶ **Workbook** page 47, exercises 6–7

Study tip!

Think about your reader when you are writing. Make your text interesting. Add some personal information and your feelings.

8 Think of a street you know well. Write about it.

1 What places are there on the street?

2 Are they important for you? Why?

3 Write about the street. Check your work carefully.

4 Write your text neatly and add a picture.

 EXTRA Solve the puzzle.

Mum, Dad, Sam and Sue want a new house. Dad works in a hospital and Mum works in a café. Sam and Sue go to swimming classes. Which is the perfect street in exercise 3 for the family?

YOU FIRST! What do you like at the funfair?

1 a 🔊 **3.06** ▶ Read and listen to the story. Who doesn't like funfairs?

b Read the story again. Answer the questions.

1 Does Chris like ghost trains?
2 Who loves trampolines?
3 Can Finn catch Chris?
4 Can they see Chris?
5 Do the children want a hot dog?
6 Does the coconut shy man give them Chris?
7 Do they rescue Chris from the coconut shy?
8 Where is Chris at the end of the story?

Vocabulary

2 a 🔊 **3.07** **Look at the first picture of the story. Listen and repeat the words.**

> **1** big wheel **2** ghost train **3** roller coaster
> **4** hot-dog stand **5** trampoline **6** dodgems
> **7** coconut shy **8** candyfloss stand

b Ask the other students about the funfair attractions. Can you find three people who think the same as you?

> Do you like the big wheel?

> Yes, I love it. Do you?

> No, I hate it.

> **Workbook** page 48, exercises 1–2

Grammar Prepositions of place

3 Look at the story again and complete the dialogues.

Finn Where are the trampolines?
Lily Over there! They're **¹**___ the dodgems.

Lily Excuse me. Where's the coconut shy?
Mrs Stokes It's **²**___ the candyfloss stand.
Finn Thanks! Come on! Let's go.

> You can give the position of something with **behind** and **opposite**.

4 a 🔊 **3.08** **Listen and repeat.**

> Here are some more words you can use to give positions.

in	on	under
next to	near	between
behind	in front of	opposite

b Look at the map and complete the dialogues.

A Excuse me. Where's the hot dog stand?
B It's over there. It's **¹**___ the roller coaster and the dodgems.

A Excuse me. Where are the dodgems?
B They're **²**___ the ghost train.

c Over to you! **Invent some more dialogues. Practise them with a partner.**

Look!

We say how near a thing is like this:

| here | there | over there |

> **Workbook** page 49, exercises 3–4

Speaking

5 Get ready to speak **Draw a simple fairground map with six attractions. Number the attractions 1–6**

6 Work with a partner. Ask your partner about their map and try to draw their fairground.

> Is there a roller coaster in your funfair?

> Yes, there is.

> Where is it?

 EXTRA How many words can you make with the letters in roller coaster?

ROLLER C<u>OA</u>S<u>T</u>E<u>R</u>   cat

5C The chase

How many different kinds of transport can you think of in one minute?

Vocabulary

1 a Complete the labels with the words in the box.

boat bus car

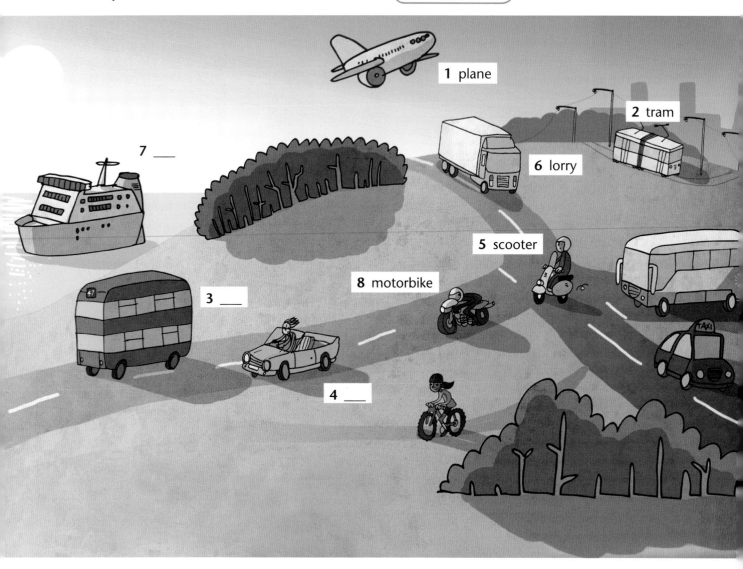

1 plane

2 tram

6 lorry

7 ___

5 scooter

8 motorbike

3 ___

4 ___

b 🔊 **3.09** Listen and check, then repeat.

2 a Look at the picture and complete the dialogue.

> Has it got wheels?

> It's got six or eight wheels.

> Is it red?

> No, it isn't.

> I know. It's the ___ .

b 🔊 **3.10** Listen and check, then repeat.

c Over to you! Work with a partner. Ask and answer questions about the picture.

Study tip!

Guessing games are good speaking practice. Play guessing games with your friends about animals, food, people, etc.

▶ **Workbook** page 50, exercises 1–3

Reading and Grammar

Present simple: *Wh*- questions

3 a 🔊 **3.11** Read and listen to the story about agent Jane P. How many vehicles are there in the story?

A day in the life of Jane P, Agent 077

Jane P is in her car. Jane has got a secret code in her mobile phone. It can save the world from the aliens. SuperSpy HQ needs Jane. They need her now!

A motorbike stops next to Jane's car. The rider points his finger at Jane's window, and it opens. Jane looks at them – they aren't people; they're aliens!

The passenger points at Jane's mobile phone. It flies out of the window and into the alien's hand. Then he points at Jane's car. Suddenly the car stops!

There's a man on a scooter in front of Jane's car. Jane borrows the scooter and follows the aliens. But the scooter is slow, and the aliens are going fast!

There's a lorry on the bridge. It stops. The aliens can't pass it. They jump off the bridge and onto a boat on the river. They're scared now. Water is dangerous for these aliens.

b Read the story again. Match the questions and answers about the story.

1 **Who** does HQ need?
2 **Where** does the motorbike stop?
3 **What** does the first alien take?
4 **Why** can't the aliens cross the bridge?
5 **Where** do the aliens jump?

a Onto a boat.
b Because there is a lorry on the bridge.
c Next to Jane's car.
d Jane's mobile phone.
e Jane P.

4 Look at the answers in exercise 3b and complete the rules with *places, people, reasons* and *things*.

a We use *who* to ask about ___ .
b We use *what* to ask about ___ .
c We use *where* to ask about ___ .
d We use *why* to ask about ___ .

> When we ask with *why*, we can answer with *because*.

5 Put the words in the correct order to make questions.

1 Jane What jump onto does ?
   What does Jane jump onto?
2 does Who Agent 077 follow ?
3 fall Where do the aliens ?
4 from the plane What see do they ?
5 does Why into the river Jane jump ?

> **Workbook** page 51, exercises 4–5

Speaking and Listening

6 Get ready to speak Imagine how the story ends. Answer the questions in exercise 5.

7 Work in small groups. Tell your friends your ideas.

8 🔊 **3.12** Listen to the end of the story. Are your answers correct?

> **Workbook** page 51, exercises 6–7

EXTRA Design and describe the aliens' car.

What takeaway food do you like?

1 a 🔊 **3.13** Read and listen to the story. What does Leila eat?

Rosie I'm really tired. What's the time?

Leila One o'clock. It's lunchtime.

Joel OK. Let's go to the chippy.

Rosie But I don't like fish and chips.

Leila And I don't like fried food! I want a salad!

Joel Don't worry. They've got lots of other things.

Leila Oh, OK. Let's go.

Assistant Good afternoon. What would you like?

Joel Can I have a burger and a big bag of chips, please?

Rosie I'd like a sausage in batter and a small bag of chips.

Leila A sausage in batter! Yuck! Can I have a salad, please?

Assistant Chips? Scotch egg?

Leila Oh no. No, thanks. Just salad, please.

Assistant Wait a minute, please. You're number 61.

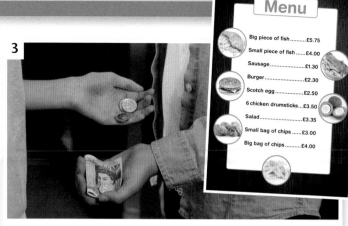

Menu	
Big piece of fish	£5.75
Small piece of fish	£4.00
Sausage	£1.30
Burger	£2.30
Scotch egg	£2.50
6 chicken drumsticks	£3.50
Salad	£3.35
Small bag of chips	£3.00
Big bag of chips	£4.00

Joel How much is the sausage and chips, Rosie?

Rosie A sausage is £1.30 and the chips are £3.00. So that's £4.30.

Joel My burger and chips is £6.30. How much is the salad, Leila?

Leila £3.35.

Assistant Order number 61!

Rosie Thanks. How much is it?

Assistant That's £13.95, please.

Rosie Here you are. £14.00.

Assistant And here's your change.

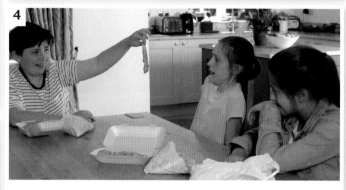

Joel Where's my burger? I'm hungry!

Rosie Here you are. And these are your chips.

Joel Thanks.

Rosie This is my sausage…and these are my chips…oh.

Leila What's the matter?

Rosie I can't see your salad. It isn't in the bag.

Leila Oh no. I'm hungry! I'm starving!

Joel Look, there's some salad in my burger. Would you like it?

Leila Um, no thanks Joel. But…can I share your chips?

b Read the story again. Answer the questions.

1 Why are they hungry?

2 Have they got salad at the fish and chip shop?

3 What do Rosie, Joel and Leila order?

4 What's the problem with their order?

Vocabulary

2 🔊 **3.14** **Listen and repeat.**

> We say *1p*, *2p*, etc., up to *99p*. Then we say one **pound**, two **pounds**, etc.

> We don't say *five pounds fifty p*. We say *five pounds fifty*.

Look!

This is the sign for pounds: **£**

▶ **Workbook** page 52, exercise 1

Everyday English

3 a **Look at the menu board in the story. Match the questions (1–4) to the answers (a–d).**

1 How much are the sausages?
2 How much is a bag of chips?
3 How much are the chicken drumsticks?
4 How much is a big piece of fish?

a £5.75.   c £3.50 for six.

b They're £1.30 each.   d £3.00 for a small bag.

b 🔊 **3.15** **Listen and check, then repeat.**

c **Match the sentence halves to complete the rules.**

1 We say, 'How much is…?'
2 We say, 'How much are…?'
3 We say, 'Here you are.'
4 We say, 'Thank you.'
5 We say, 'Here's your change.'

a when we receive something.
b when we give something.
c to ask the price of one thing.
d when we give change.
e to ask the price of more than one thing.

▶ **Workbook** page 52, exercises 2–3

Listening

4 a 🔊 **3.16** **Look at the menu and listen to the dialogues. Answer the questions.**

Fred's chippy

Fish:	small piece	£4.30
	big piece	£6.00
Chips:	small bag	£3.25
	big bag	£4.00
Sausage:		£1.45 each
Chicken drumsticks:		£3.50 for 6

1 What does Mum want?
2 What does Dad want?
3 What does Ben want?
4 What does Lexi want?

b **Look at the menu again. How much is the total price of the meal?**

c Over to you! **Work with a partner. Ask the prices of the things at Fred's chippy.**

Speaking

5 a Get ready to speak **Put the lines of the dialogue in the correct order.**

Assistant	Hello. Can I help you?	1
Boy	Thanks. I'd like a small piece of fish, and chips, please.	☐
Boy	How much is the fish?	☐
Assistant	What about you?	☐
Girl	Yes, please. A small bag.	☐
Assistant	£4.30 for a small piece; £6.00 for a big piece.	☐
Assistant	Would you like some chips, too?	☐
Girl	Can I have six chicken drumsticks, please?	☐
Girl	I'm not sure. How much are the chicken drumsticks?	☐
Assistant	And here's your change.	☐
Boy	Here you are. Thanks.	☐
Assistant	£3.50 for six.	☐
Assistant	Here you are. That's £15.05.	☐

b 🔊 **3.17** **Listen and check.**

6 **Do a role-play at a fish and chip shop. Use the dialogue to help you.**

 Make a menu for a takeaway shop. It can be real or imaginary.

Story

Read the story on page 53 of the Workbook and do the exercises.

Unit 5 · In town 69

Vocabulary and Grammar

1 Look at the map and write sentences. Use *next to*, *near*, *between*, *behind*, *in front of* and *opposite*.

1 school/restaurant
2 man/museum
3 museum/school
4 library/supermarket
5 car/school
6 shopping centre/ swimming pool
7 café/shopping centre/museum

2 Label the pictures.

1 ___
2 ___
3 ___
4 ___
5 ___
6 ___
7 ___
8 ___

3 Write the questions for the answers. Use *What*, *Why*, *Where* and *Who...with*.

1 Where does Ryan go?   He goes **to the fair**.
2 ___ ?   He goes **with his friend Becca**.
3 ___ ?   He loves **the big wheel**.
4 ___ the big wheel?   **Because** he can see the town from the air.

4 Write sentences about the picture with *There is/isn't* and *There are/aren't*. Use the words in the box.

> boat ~~buses~~ cars lorries
> motorbikes plane scooters tram

There are some buses.

Everyday English

5 a Write the questions.

1   2   3   4

1 How much *is* a piece of fish?

b Complete the dialogue.

> ~~Can~~ Do you here's your change
> Here you are How much are
> How much is that I'd

Waitress Good morning. ¹Can I help you?
Boy Yes, please. ²___ like two Scotch eggs, please.
Waitress ³___ want some chips, too?
Boy Yes, please. ⁴___ the chips?
Waitress A small bag is £3.25. A big bag is £4.00.
Boy I'd like a small bag of chips, and a salad, too.
Waitress ⁵___ .
Boy Thanks. ⁶___ ?
Waitress £10.15, please.
Boy Here you are. £11.00.
Waitress Thank you. And ⁷___ .

▶ **Workbook** pages 54–55, exercises 1–6

Imagine a street with your favourite places on it. What are they?

Make a POP-UP of your PERFECT STREET

A

B

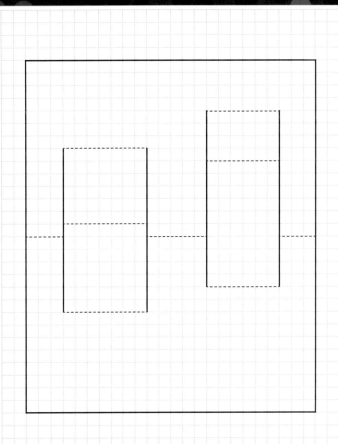

1 Look at the projects. Do they have the same places on their streets?

2 Which project are the sentences about?

  a There's a restaurant and a school on my perfect street.

  b We can walk to the restaurant from the school.

  c There's a swimming pool because I love sports.

  d There's an Italian restaurant because I like pizzas.

  e There isn't a museum because I don't like museums.

3 Which project is very good? Which project needs more work?

Study tip!

You can learn a lot from other people's work. Look carefully at good examples and think about why they are successful.

4 Now create your own pop-up street.

  1 Copy the template above onto an A4 card or paper.

  2 Think of four places for your street. Why do you want these places?

  3 Draw your places on your street.

  4 Make the pop-up street.

  5 Prepare notes for your presentation.

5 a Present your pop-up street to the class. Tell your class about your street.

  b Listen to your friends. Ask a question.

What famous bridges do you know? Where are they?

FAMOUS BRIDGES

Name:	Tarr Steps
Place:	This bridge is in a national park in the UK, called Exmoor.
Age:	Historians can't say the age of the bridge. Some people say it is 3,000 years old.
Length:	It is 55 metres long.
Interesting fact:	All the stones have a number on them. When there is a lot of water in the river, the bridge breaks. They build the bridge again. They use the numbers to put the stones in the correct order.

Name:	Tower Bridge
Place:	This bridge is in London, in the UK. It crosses the River Thames.
Age:	The bridge opened in 1894.
Length:	It is 244 metres long.
Interesting fact:	The top bridge is for people. The bottom bridge is for traffic. The bottom bridge opens about 800 times every year for boats to pass.

Name:	Golden Gate Bridge
Place:	This bridge is in San Francisco, in the USA. It crosses the point where San Francisco Bay meets the Pacific Ocean.
Age:	The bridge opened in 1937.
Length:	It is 2,737 metres long.
Interesting fact:	The bridge isn't gold – it's orange. There is a lot of fog in San Francisco. Orange is easy to see in the fog.

Name:	Coaticook Gorge Suspension Bridge
Place:	This bridge crosses the Coaticook River in Quebec, Canada. It is the longest suspended footbridge in the world.
Age:	The bridge opened in 1988.
Length:	It is 80 metres long.
Interesting fact:	The bridge is only 2 metres wide. About 800 people can cross the bridge at the same time. It's scary: you can see the river 130 metres under the bridge!

1 Look at the photos in the leaflets. Where are the bridges?

2 a Choose a bridge. Read about it. Then answer the questions.
1 What's its name?
2 How old is it?
3 How long is it?
4 What's interesting about it?

b Work in small groups. Ask your friends about the other bridges. Use the questions in 2a.

3 Over to you! Discuss in your group.
1 Are there any famous bridges in your area?
2 What are their names?
3 How long are they?

▶ Video Small town, big city

Learn through English

 YOU FIRST! What is a good place to build a town?

From
VILLAGE to TOWN

Towns change and grow over the years. History and technology change towns.

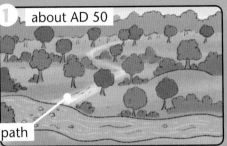

1 about AD 50

path

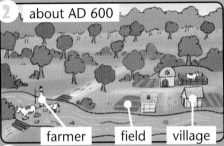

2 about AD 600

farmer   field   village

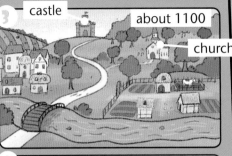

castle

3 about 1100

church

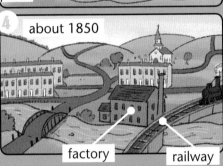

4 about 1850

factory   railway

5 about 1970

6 about 2010

block of flats

A It's about AD 50.

There's a forest and there's a river. There aren't any houses or shops, but there's a path. People use the stones to cross the river.

B It's ___ .

The town is very big now. There are shops, parks and schools. There are big houses on the edge of the town. There are lots of cars on the roads.

C It's ___ .

The town is big now. There isn't a castle. There's a railway and factories. People don't work on the farms: they work in the factories. There are lots of small houses for the factory workers.

D It's ___ .

There aren't any factories near the river now. There's a shopping centre and a sports centre in their place. Some people live in tall blocks of flats. There aren't any cars in the centre of town.

E It's ___ .

Now it's a small village. Farmers live in houses near the river. There are fields with plants and animals. People and animals cross the river now. There are logs on the banks to help them.

F It's ___ .

Now it's a town. It's got a castle and a church. There's a bridge over the river. There are fields near the town. At this time in history, there are a lot of wars. When there is a war, farmers go inside the city.

---

1 Read the introduction and look at the pictures. How many years of change can you see?

2 Look at the pictures again and complete the titles of the paragraphs with the date.

3 Work with a partner. Student **A** closes the book. Student **B** describes a picture. Student **A** guesses the picture.

> It's got factories, but there isn't a shopping centre.

> I know. It's about 1970.

4 Work with a partner and answer the questions.

  1 What can you see in your town from…?
    a about 1970
    b about 1850
    c about 1100

  2 How are the new parts of your town different from the old parts?

🔊 **3.18** ▶ **Song** This is my town

6 At the weekend

6A Going for a walk

 YOU FIRST! What are you wearing today?

It's snowing.

It's cold.

It's sunny.

It's hot.

It's cloudy.

It's wet.

c He's playing with a dog, and she's playing a video game. They're wearing white T-shirts. He's got brown shorts, and she's got a pink skirt. They've got flip-flops on their feet.

a She's playing with a dog, and he's taking a photo. They're wearing red jumpers. He's got a red hat, and she's got a black scarf.

b He's got short, dark hair, and she's got long, fair hair. They're wearing blue trousers and black shoes. His jacket is black, and her jacket is green.

Vocabulary

1 a Look at the pictures and read the descriptions. Match the clothes to the numbers in the pictures.

___ flip-flops ___ hat ___ jacket ___ jumper 1 scarf
___ shoes ___ shorts ___ skirt ___ trousers ___ T-shirt

b 🔊 **3.19** Listen and check, then repeat.

2 a 🔊 **3.20** Look at the pictures in exercise 1a. Complete the speech bubbles. Then listen and check.

> He's wearing black trousers.

> He's wearing black trousers, and his ___ is red.

> He's wearing black trousers, his ___ is red, and he's got ___ hair.

> He's wearing black trousers, his ___ is red, he's got ___ hair, and his hair is ___ .

b Work with a partner. Play the *Make a long sentence* game.

Remember!

He's got a big hat.
His hat is red.
She's got brown hair.
Her hair is short.

▶ **Workbook** page 56, exercises 1–3

Listening and Grammar *What...like?*

3 a 🔊 **3.21** Listen to four episodes of a TV show. Match the episodes (1–4) to the pictures (a–d).

a

Evie at the North Pole

b

Evie in the Amazon

c

Evie on Everest

d

Evie on Bondi Beach

b 🔊 **3.21** Listen again. Answer the questions.

Episode 1 What can Evie see? ___

Episode 2 Why does she need long trousers and strong shoes? ___

Episode 3 Is everything perfect? ___

Episode 4 What can't Evie see? ___

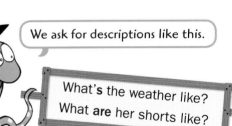

We ask for descriptions like this.

What's the weather like?
What **are** her shorts like?

4 a Look at the pictures of Evie and complete the dialogues with the place.

1 A What's the weather like?
 B It's cold and it's snowing.
 A I know. She's ___ .

2 A What are her trousers like?
 B They're long and green.
 A I know. She's ___ .

b 🔊 **3.22** Listen and check.

c Work in pairs. Ask and answer about the pictures.

d Over to you! What's the weather like today for you?

▶ **Workbook** pages 56–57, exercises 4–5

Reading and Writing

5 a Look at the pictures in exercise 3a. Read the texts and find the false sentence in each text. Correct the false sentences.

A Evie is going for a walk in the Amazon. It's hot and it's wet. She's wearing long, green shorts, a white T-shirt, a big hat and strong shoes. She's going down a zip wire. She can't stop. There's a snake on the tree at the end. It's waiting for her.

B Evie is going for a walk at the North Pole. It's cold and it's snowing. She's wearing black trousers, a big, orange jacket, strong shoes and a short scarf. There are two polar bears near her – they're hungry. It's lunchtime for polar bears!

Study tip!

Imagination is important when you are reading.
Make a picture in your mind when reading descriptions.

b Complete the notes about Evie.

	A	B
Where is Evie?	the Amazon	the North Pole
What's the weather like?		
What are her clothes like?		
What's the problem?		

6 Get ready to write Make notes for a new *Evie the Explorer* programme. Use the questions in exercise 5b to help you.

▶ **Workbook** page 57, exercises 6–7

7 Write the introduction for your new *Evie the Explorer* programme.

EXTRA

Write six sentences about the weather and your clothes for different months of the year.

YOU FIRST! **What do you do on wet days?**

1 a 🔊 **3.23** ▶ **Read and listen to the story. Where is Sid?**

b Read the story again. Answer the questions.

1 What's the weather like?

2 What are Finn and Lily doing in the shopping centre?

3 Who can Chris see?

4 What are they doing in the sports show?

5 Where is the reporter?

6 Who is she talking to?

7 What's he looking at?

8 Why is Sid in the pizza box?

Vocabulary

2 a Complete the labels with the words in the box.

> cookery show   documentary   game show
> music show   nature programme

1 ___

2 cartoon

3 film

4 series

5 ___

6 ___

7 comedy

8 ___

9 sports programme

10 the news

11 ___

12 talent show

b 🔊 **3.24** Listen and check, then repeat.

c Over to you! Ask other students about the TV programmes they watch. Can you find three people who watch the same as you?

▶ **Workbook** page 58, exercises 1–3

Pronunciation /r/ silent r

3 🔊 **3.25** Listen and repeat.

Where's the remote? What's on TV?
Zap, zap, zap. What can we see?

A nature show about rare buffalos,
A cartoon with a rat and two mice,
A romantic film of a rock'n'roll band,
And a cookery show about rice.

▶ **Workbook** page 58, exercise 4

Grammar

Present continuous: review

4 a Look at the story. Who says the sentences?

1 A documentary about Madagascar.
2 I don't know! Are they riding bikes?
3 Chef Luigi from Don Luigi's.
4 That! There's a snake in my pizza box.

> Look at these questions with **talk to**, **look for** and **look at**.

> Who are you talking **to**?
> What are you looking **for**?
> What are you looking **at**?

b Find the questions for the answers in 4a.

c How do we make the present continuous? Choose the correct ending to make the rule.

We make the present continuous with *am / is / are* + …

a verb + *-ing*   **b** verb   **c** verb + *s*

d When do we use the present continuous? Choose the correct ending to make the rule.

We use the present continuous to talk about…

a things we like   **b** routines   **c** now

5 a Look at the pictures in exercise 2. What are they doing? Choose a verb and a noun from the clouds to make six sentences.

> climb   do
> draw   drive
> make   play x 2
> ride   look at
> talk about
> talk to   watch

> a cake   a crocodile
> a famous person
> a horse   a lorry   a pyramid
> a snake   a teacher   a tree
> basketball
> judo   the guitar

1 She's drawing a crocodile.

b Work with a partner. Student **A** says a sentence. Student **B** says the programme.

▶ **Workbook** page 59, exercises 5–6

Speaking

6 Get ready to speak Work with a partner. Prepare eight sets of sentences for the *Drawing game*.

e.g.: She's in a music show. She's singing.

7 Work in small groups. Take turns to give a sentence to another team. One student draws the sentences. The students guess them.

> Is she in the talent show?   Yes, she is.

> Is she eating?   No, she isn't.

> Is she singing?   Yes, she is. Now it's your turn.

EXTRA Write three important things to remember about the present continuous.

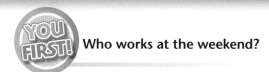

Who works at the weekend?

Vocabulary

1 a Complete the labels with the words in the box.

bus driver   doctor   musician   teacher

1 ___

2 nurse

3 ___

4 scientist

5 shop assistant

6 flight attendant

7 police officer

8 hairdresser

9 ___

10 reporter

11 mechanic

12 ___

13 film director

14 artist

b 🔊 **3.26** Listen and check, then repeat.

2 Work with a partner. Mime a job for your partner to guess.

Are you a police officer?

No, I'm not.

Are you a flight attendant?

Yes, I am.

▶ **Workbook** page 60, exercises 1–2

Reading and Grammar

Present simple: review and extension

3 a Read the descriptions. Match the photos (1–4) to the texts (a–b).

1 DIRECTOR
2
3
4

a My dad is a film director. He works for a company that makes animal documentaries. He doesn't make documentaries about elephants or lions. He makes films about very small animals. His favourite animals are spiders. He says they are amazing. There are thousands of different kinds of spider, and they are all very interesting. When he makes a film, he works seven days a week.

b My mum is an artist. She doesn't paint pictures; she works in a film studio. Every film needs different things. She makes things like puppets, robots and masks. My mum makes models of food, too! It is hot in the studio, and they can't use real food. Her food looks fantastic! Mum works Monday to Friday. She doesn't work at the weekend.

b Read the texts again and answer the questions.

Dad

1 What does he do?
2 Who does he work for?
3 What does he make films about?
4 What are his favourite animals?
5 Does he work at weekends?

Mum

1 What does she do?
2 Does she paint pictures?
3 What does she make?
4 Why does she make models of food?
5 Does she work at the weekend?

We ask about jobs like this.

What does he/she do?

4 a Who says the sentences, Dad or Mum?

1 I work seven days a week.

2 I make puppets, masks and robots.

3 I don't paint pictures.

4 I don't make films about elephants or lions.

> We use the **present simple** to talk about what we do at work.

b Choose the correct answer for the rules about the present simple.

1 We add an 's' to the verb in third person singular sentences (*he, she, it*)…

  a in the positive

  b in the negative

  c in questions

2 We make questions with…

  a *am, are* or *is*

  b *can*

  c *do* or *does*

3 We make negatives with…

  a *can't*

  b *don't* or *doesn't*

  c *aren't* or *isn't*

Study tip!

Teaching is a good way of learning. Think about how to explain the present simple to a student in the year below you.

c Use the correct form of the verbs in brackets to make sentences.

1 I'm a doctor. (✗ work in a leisure centre / ✓ work in a hospital)

  I don't work in a leisure centre; I work in a hospital.

2 She's a teacher. (✗ teach Maths/✓ teach English)

3 They're hairdressers. (✗ wash clothes/✓ cut hair)

4 He's a nurse. (✗ wear his own clothes/ ✓ wear a uniform)

5 I'm a driver. (✗ drive a lorry/✓ drive a bus)

6 She's a police officer. (✗ sit at a desk/✓ drive a car)

7 He's a musician. (✗ play the violin/ ✓ play the guitar)

8 They're scientists. (✗ study plants/✓ study animals)

▶ **Workbook** pages 60–61, exercises 3–4

Listening

5 a 🔊 **3.27 Listen to the game show *What's the job*? What are the jobs they guess?**

GUESS THEIR JOBS!

500

b 📝 **Write the questions the contestants ask. Use the words in the boxes.**

Does she work in a school?

> drive   play   wear   work x3   work with

> a bus   a musical instrument   at night
> at weekends   a uniform   ~~in a school~~
> in a supermarket   people

c 🔊 **3.28 Listen again and check.**

Speaking

6 a Get ready to speak Complete the dialogue for a flight attendant.

A Does he work in a hospital?

B No, he doesn't.

A Does he wear a uniform?

B ___ .

A Does he work with people?

B ___ .

A Does he work at night?

B ___ .

A Does he work on a plane?

B ___ .

A I know! He's a flight attendant.

b 🔊 **3.29 Listen and check.**

c Practise the dialogue with a partner.

7 Work in small groups. Play the *What's the job?* game. Use the questions in exercises 5 and 6 to help you. Remember, you can only ask *yes/no* questions.

Use your dictionary. Find out how to say jobs your family and friends do.

Where do you meet your friends at the weekend?

1 a 🔊 **3.30** ▶ **Read and listen to the story. What is on at the cinema?**

1

Jan	Hi Rosie!
Rosie	Hi. There's a superheroes special at Cinema City this afternoon.
Jan	Great! I love superheroes. I've got a Batman costume!
Rosie	Cool! Can you text Leila? I haven't got much credit.
Jan	Sure. What's her phone number?
Rosie	It's 07700 985329.
Jan	Thanks. See you later.

2

Jan: Do you want 👁 🦸 🕷 🐱 ?

Leila: 🙂 What time ?

Jan: 5.30 🎬 🏢 Come in costume!

Leila: 👍 See you! ✋

3

Leila	Rosie! Is that you?
Rosie	Yes, it is. Where are you?
Leila	I'm at the wildlife park. I'm waiting for you!
Rosie	At the wildlife park! We're at the cinema.
Leila	The cinema? But there aren't any animals at the cinema.
Rosie	Animals? Why are you talking about animals?! There's a superheroes special at Cinema City – Batman, Spider-Man and Catwoman.
Leila	Oh! Now I understand Jan's text! I'm on the way!

b Read the story again. Answer the questions.

1 What costume has Jan got?
2 Why can't Rosie call Leila?

3 Does Leila understand Jan's messages?
4 Why does Leila go to the wildlife park?

Vocabulary

2  **3.31** Listen and repeat.

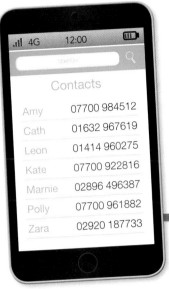

.ıll 4G   12:00

Contacts

Amy	07700 984512
Cath	01632 967619
Leon	01414 960275
Kate	07700 922816
Marnie	02896 496387
Polly	07700 961882
Zara	02920 187733

We say phone numbers like this:
oh – double seven – double oh – nine – eight – four – five – one – two

We say double numbers like this.

33 = double three
BUT
00 = double oh

3 a Complete the dialogue.

A Oh – double seven – double oh – nine – six – one – double eight – two.

B That's ____'s number.

b  **3.32** Listen and check.

c Work with a partner. Student **A** says a number and Student **B** says whose number it is.

▶ **Workbook** page 62, exercise 1

Everyday English

4 a Who says the sentences in the story?

1 What's her phone number?

2 Rosie! Is that you?

3 It's 07700 985329.

b Match the rules (a–c) to the sentences (1–3) in exercise 4a.

a You ask for a phone number like this.

b You give a phone number like this.

c You ask who is calling like this.

c  **3.33** Listen and check, then repeat.

Here are some alternative phrases.

Hello, who's that? = Hi, who's calling?
It's Rosie! = Rosie here.
Bye. = Goodbye.
Thanks for the message. = Thanks for calling.

▶ **Workbook** page 62, exercises 2–3

Listening

5  **3.34** Listen to the phone calls and match the top halves (1–3) to the bottom halves (a–c) of the sticky notes.

1 Remember!

2 Meet Ed this afternoon.

3 Message from Paula for Kay

a Sports Centre/5.30

b Call her: 07700 918735

c Your guitar class is at 6.00.

Speaking

6 Get ready to speak Work with a partner. Choose a note and invent the phone conversation for it.

Remember!
Football at 5.30 this afternoon.

Meet Tina after school.

Message from Dave to Raj. Please call your mum.

Don't forget! Buy some ice cream at the supermarket.

7 a Present your conversation to the class.

b Listen to other students' conversations. Choose the note for their conversations.

EXTRA Imagine you are organizing a party. Write three phone messages you can leave for your friends.

Story

Read the story on page 63 of the Workbook and do the exercises.

Vocabulary and Grammar

1 Look at the pictures and correct the sentences.

1 He's wearing shorts.

He isn't wearing shorts. He's wearing trousers.

2 He's wearing flip-flops.

3 Her T-shirt is white.

4 They're wearing red hats.

5 He's got a blue scarf.

2 Make questions and answers about the weather on the island.

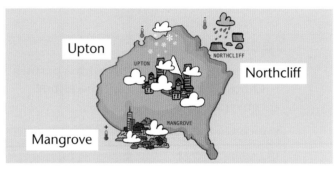

Upton

Northcliff

Mangrove

1 What's the weather like in Upton today?

It's cold and it's snowing.

2 (Northcliffe)   3 (Mongrove)

3 Write questions and answers about Aaron and Alice. What do they watch at the weekend? Do they like it?

	Aaron	Alice
🖥️	✓ 😎	✓ 👍
🖥️	✗ 👎	✗ 👎
🖥️	✗ 😕	✗ 👎
🖥️	✓ 👍	✓ 👍

1 Aaron/cartoons

Does Aaron watch cartoons?

Yes, he does. He loves them.

2 Aaron and Alice/cookery shows

3 Alice/documentaries

4 Aaron and Alice/music shows

4 Write questions and answers about their jobs.

1 What do they do?

They're flight attendants.

Everyday English

5 Complete the phone conversation.

A Hello! ¹___ that?

B ²___ Suzie.

A Oh, hi Suzie.

B ³___ give me Tony's mobile number?

A Yes, of course. ⁴___ 07700 962187.

B Thanks.

A OK. Bye.

B ⁵___ .

▶ **Workbook** pages 64–65, exercises 1–6

Design a uniform

a These big pockets are for their snacks. Aliens don't eat British food. They need their special alien food.

b These are trousers and shorts. They know that the weather in Britain changes every day.

c These reporters are aliens. They are visiting Britain. This is their uniform.

d The aliens can choose the colours of their uniform.

e This pocket is for their cameras and mobile phones.

f They can run fast with these shoes. They are scared of people. They think they aren't friendly.

g The bag is for useful things. It's got a football, a guitar and some soap. The aliens watch British TV adverts. They know people in Britain like football, music and clean clothes.

1 a Look at the project. Describe the reporters' uniforms.

b Read the notes (a–g) and match them to the correct parts of the picture (1–7).

2 Look at the project again. Tick (✔) the sentences which are true for a good project.

1 The uniform has got some special features.
2 You can see uniforms for men and women.
3 The sticky notes give extra information.
4 The poster shows the colours of the uniform.
5 The poster gives the price of the uniform.

3 Over to you! Design a uniform for human explorers visiting an alien planet. Answer the questions and prepare your project.

1 Who is your uniform for?
2 What is the alien planet like? Think about the weather, the animals, the food, etc.
3 Look at examples of uniforms on the internet or in books.
4 How can you make your uniform interesting and useful?
5 What colour is your uniform?
6 What can you write about your uniform?

4 a Show and explain your uniform to the class.

b Listen to your classmates. Ask questions.

Why has the uniform got a big hat?

Because it protects explorers from the three suns on the planet.

Are there any special days in summer in your country?

Special days in summer

How do you celebrate Independence Day?

float

Americans celebrate Independence Day on 4th July. The celebration is more than 200 years old. Here are some of the answers to our question.

Ashley

We have a barbecue in our garden. We decorate the garden with the American flag. We eat hot dogs, burgers and apple pie. At night, we have fireworks – red, white and blue fireworks, of course!

Tyler

We go to Washington, DC. There are red, white and blue decorations in the streets. We watch the parade. I love the bands, and the floats are fantastic. We go to the concert and the fireworks in the evening.

What's your favourite part of the Notting Hill Carnival?

parade

Notting Hill is in London. They have a Caribbean Carnival on the last weekend of August. It is a big party! Here are some answers to our question.

Darrell

I love the J'ouvert. It starts at six o'clock on Sunday morning. We wear very old clothes because you get very dirty at the J'ouvert. People throw flour, paint and chocolate! We follow the parade of ghosts and monsters, and we sing and dance. It's fun!

Blake

The food stalls are my favourite part of the Carnival. They make jerk chicken on a barbecue. It's delicious! You can buy coconut water, too. They make a hole in the coconut, and you drink the water with a straw!

Glossary

barbecue

fireworks

coconut + straw

1 **Look at the pictures of Independence Day and Notting Hill Carnival. Match the words to the festivals.**

> concert   dance   dirty   flag   food stalls
> hot dogs   old clothes   red, white and blue

2 a **Choose one of the texts. Read it and check your answers to exercise 1.**

 b **Answer the questions for your text.**
 1 When is the festival?
 2 What are two things people do at the festival?
 3 What is typical food and drink at the festival?

 c **Work with a partner. Ask them about their text.**

3 a 🔊 **3.35 Listen to Lauren and Ramona. Which festival are they each talking about?**

 b 🔊 **3.35 Listen again and answer the questions.**
 Lauren
 1 Where is the picnic?
 2 What do they eat?
 3 What does Lauren's mum make?
 4 What do they do after the picnic?

 Ramona
 1 What's her favourite day of the festival? Why?
 2 What do they do in the parade?
 3 Do they listen to pop music?

4 **Over to you! Answer the questions.**
 1 Which festival would you like to go to?
 2 What would you like to do?
 3 Answer the questions in exercise 2b for a summer festival in your area.

▶ **Video** A summer festival

YOU FIRST! How do we change in summer and winter? Think about clothes, activities and food.

Animals and their habitats

dustbin

woods

a

Some **European foxes** live in woods and some live in cities. Their fur is red-brown. They eat plants and small animals. There isn't a lot of food in the woods for foxes in the winter.

grassland

b **Arctic foxes** live in cold places. They are white in winter and brown in summer. They've got small ears, short legs and thick fur. Arctic foxes eat small animals. They listen for the animals under the snow. Then they jump up and catch them.

desert

c

Fennec foxes live in the desert in North Africa. They've got light brown fur, big ears and big eyes. The foxes sleep in a hole in the ground in the day. At night, the foxes wake up and find small animals to eat.

1 a **Look at the photos of the foxes. Which fox lives in the desert, the Arctic, the woods or a city?**

b **Match the sentence halves.**

1 It's hot in the day and cold at night
2 There's snow in winter and grass in summer
3 The trees are green in winter and brown in summer
4 There's food in the dustbins in winter and summer

a in a city.
b in the woods.
c in the desert.
d in the Arctic.

2 a **Read about the foxes. Answer the questions for each fox.**

1 Where do they live?
2 What colour are they?
3 What do they eat?

b **Work with a partner. Which fox or foxes are the sentences about?**

1 The colour of its coat is the same as the colour of the place it lives.
2 It can find food in bins in the city.
3 It uses its ears to find its food.
4 It jumps to break the snow.
5 It sleeps in the day to escape the sun.

3 **Over to you!** **Work with a partner and discuss the questions.**

1 Which other animals change colour in summer and winter?
2 Which other animals are the same colour as the place they live?
3 Which other animals have special body parts to help them find food?

1 🔊 3.36 ▶ Read and listen to the story.

OXFORD
UNIVERSITY PRESS

Great Clarendon Street, Oxford, OX2 6DP, United Kingdom

Oxford University Press is a department of the University of Oxford.
It furthers the University's objective of excellence in research, scholarship,
and education by publishing worldwide. Oxford is a registered trade
mark of Oxford University Press in the UK and in certain other countries

© Oxford University Press 2019

The moral rights of the author have been asserted

First published in 2019

2023 2022 2021 2020 2019

10 9 8 7 6 5 4 3 2 1

ISBN: 978 0 19 425569 1

Printed in China

This book is printed on paper from certified and well-managed sources

ACKNOWLEDGEMENTS

Based on an original concept by Tom Hutchinson

Doctor Z by: Paul Shipton (pp.34 -35, 60 -61, 86 -87)

Songs written and composed by: Jake Carter

The authors and publishers are very grateful to all the teachers who have offered their comments and suggestions which have been invaluable in the development of Project Explore. We would particularly like to mention those who have helped by commenting on Project Explore:

Croatia: Kristina Pirs, Martina Prpa

Czech Republic: Ludmila Balíková

Hungary: Aradi László, Nagy Eszter

Serbia: Vojislava Koljević, Jagoda Popovic

Slovakia: Eva Gambaľová, Andrea Popadicova

Slovenia: Vojko Jurgec, Adela Krois

The authors would like to thank the editorial and design teams at Oxford
University Press who have contributed their skills and ideas to producing this
course.

Front cover photograph: Mike Stone.

Back cover photograph: Oxford University Press building/David Fisher.

Commissioned photography by: MM Studios pp.6, 8, 16, 28, 42, 54, 68, 80.

Illustrations by: Mark Duffin like/dislike icons, p.31; Daniel Duncan/The Bright Group pp.9, 12, 22, 23, 29 (ex5), 38 (ex1), 44, 55, 70 (ex2), 73, 75, 83; Gareth Llewhellin/The Bright Group pp.13 (ex5), 18, 37, 62 (ex3), 65 (ex4b), 70 (ex1), 82 (ex1-3); Alex Lopez/Astound US Inc pp.4, 5, 7, 8, 9, 10, 11, 13, 14, 15, 17, 23, 25, 26, 27, 29, 37, 38, 39, 40, 41, 43, 48, 49, 50, 51, 52, 63, 64, 65, 67, 69, 75, 76, 77, 78, 79, 81; Teresa Martinez/Astound US Inc pp.7 (ex4b), 24, 25, 30 (ex5), 41, 74; Jennifer Naalchigar pp.11 (ex2), 13 (ex6), 19, 27 (ex7), 39, 47, 62 (ex1); Jamie Pogue/The Bright Group pp.8, 10, 11, 16, 17 (clocks), 20, 21, 29 (ex3b), 30 (ex1), 38, 43, 48, 51, 52, 53, 56, 59, 65 (Look!), 70 (ex4&5), 77, 79, 82 (ex4); Ben Scruton/Meiklejohn Illustration p.66; Amit Tayal/Beehive Illustration pp.34, 35, 60, 61, 67, 86, 67.

*The publisher would like to thank the following for permission to reproduce photographs:*123RF pp.12 (twenty/inkdrop), 12 (thirty/Aleksandar Varbenov), 12 (forty/megastocker), 12 (fifty/Fernando Sanchez), 12 (sixty/Micha Klootwijk), 12 (seventy/roseov), 12 (eighty/Andrii Rafalskyi), 12 (label/Ekaterina Minaeva); Alamy Stock Photo pp.13 (leaves as umbrellas/Design Pics Inc), 21 (sundial/Zoonar GmbH), 21 (The Tower Hotel Sundial/Terry Mathews), 21 (Analemmatic sundial/PjrTravel), 27 (trading card/razorpix), 27 (spider-man comic/Les Breault), 27 (car magazine/Art Directors & TRIP), 27 (smiley badge/Alex Segre), 27 (house key/filmfoto), 27 (plastic dinosaur/ Michael Burrell), 32 (mosaic serpent/Peter Horree), 32 (Egyptian Animal Mummies/Hemis), 33 (Dunnock at nest/David Hosking), 33 (little owl/Brian Bevan), 36 (school lunch/MBI), 36 (schoolboy/Photofusion Picture Library), 36 (red school bus/Colin Underhill), 45 (yellow school bus/Curtseyes), 45 (Oxford Castle/Joana Kruse), 45 (Christ Church meadow/Mark Beton/ UK), 45 (Punting on the River Cherwell/Ian Dagnall), 45 (Rhinos at Cotswold Wildlife Park/Robin Weaver), 46 (sack race/Mark Boulton), 46 (mums race/ MH People), 46 (community fete/jason freeman), 57 (solar oven/Frances Roberts), 57 (seed bombs/blickwinkel), 58 (Highland dancers/travelbild.com), 69 (Polymer five pound note/Joseph Gaul), 69 (polymer ten pound note/Alex), 69 (twenty pound note/Ben Molyneux), 72 (Tarr Steps clapper bridge/Paul Weston), 78 (prop food/Stephen Barnes/Entertainment), 85 (fox/tbkmedia. de), 85 (fox/dpa picture alliance); Daniel Holden p.21 (homemade sundial); Getty Images pp.18 (family/Simon Potter), 18 (happy girl/PeopleImages), 19 (teen boy/Erin Patrice O'Brien), 30 (schoolboy/Phil Boorman), 31 (girl with plaits/Howard Kingsnorth), 36 (sleeping boy/Sue Barr), 36 (girl tying laces/ Julie Toy), 36 (boy eating cereal/Kraig Scarbinsky), 36 (girl with apple/Natalie Faye), 36 (boy eating spaghetti/fStop Images), 36 (brushing teeth/KidStock), 36 (child sleeping/Juanmonino), 36 (girl at door/David Young-Wolff), 36 (boy studying/Elisabeth Schmitt), 36 (camp fire/Titus Lacoste), 43 (Smiling African American boy/Sam Bloomberg-Rissman), 43 (young girl/Mike Kemp), 46 (boys on tractor/Jamie Grill Photography), 57 (Eugene Cernan on Lunar Rover/ NASA/Science Photo Library), 57 (butterfly/Peter Travers/Digital Camera Magazine), 58 (bodyboarding/Justin Pumfrey), 72 (suspended footbridge/David Chapman), 78 (classroom/Caiaimage/Chris Ryan), 78 (director/bjones27), 78 (animal prop/Matt Cardy), 83 (schoolboy/Hero Images), 84 (Independence parade/Gabrielle Lurie/AFP), 84 (smiling girl/Artem Varnitsin/EyeEm), 84 (preteen boy/PhotoAlto/Frederic Cirou), 84 (Notting Hill Carnival/Daniel Leal-Olivas/AFP), 84 (young boy/Jamie Garbutt), 84 (boy outside/Kryssia Campos), 84 (girl at playground/Hero Images), 84 (mixed race girl/Kevin Dodge), 85 (Arctic fox/Wayne Lynch), 85 (Fennec fox/Konrad Wothe/Minden Pictures); Joyce Ligeti-Pretorius p.71; Oxford University Press pp.4 (pencil/ Dennis Kitchen Studio, Inc.), 4 (pencils/Africa Studio), 4 (books/ajt), 12 (ninety/ Andrew Rafalsky), 20 (flags of the world/xiver), 20 (world map/Mervana), 27 (stickers/lian_2011), 27 (ammonite/Lutya), 27 (Buzz Lightyear toy/N Azlin Sha), 41 (bananas/Gareth Boden), 41 (cheese/Kim Nguyen), 41 (eggs/ virtu studio), 41 (jam/eZeePics Studio), 43 (cupcake/Ruth Black), 43 (biscuits/ Moving Moment), 43 (popcorn/Helen Sessions), 43 (crisps/bitt24), 43 (pizza/ Africa Studio), 43 (burger/primopiano), 43 (hot dog/C Squared Studios), 43 (orange juice/Evgeny Karandaev), 43 (ice creams/Ingram), 43 (apple pie/ HG Photography), 44 (biscuits/Moving Moment), 44 (popcorn/Helen Sessions), 44 (cheese/Kim Nguyen), 44 (eggs/virtu studio), 44 (ice creams/Ingram), 46 (spoon/kritskaya), 58 (tropical beach/Efired), 62 (cinema/Radu Bercan), 62 (British Museum/Cedric Weber), 62 (pool/Tatiana Belova), 62 (cafe/Chris King), 62 (restaurant/ariadna de raadt), 62 (library/Lim Yong Hian), 68 (fish and chips/Joe Gough), 68 (burger/rvlsoft), 68 (chips/kungverylucky), 68 (wood background/Reinhold Leitner), 69 (British coins/Claudio Divizia), 69 (British pound/Craig Russell), 78 (doctor/Monkey Business Images), 78 (nurse/ Monkey Business Images), 78 (Policewoman/pcruciatti), 78 (painter/George Dolgikh), 78 (sports reporter/Maxisport), 84 (barbecue/stockcreations), 84 (fireworks/Pavel Vakhrushev); Shutterstock pp.4 (book/kak2s), 18 (family/ Ruslan Guzov), 21 (sundial/Nick Andros), 27 (souvenir magnets/Concept Photo), 28 (colourful scenes/malamalama), 28 (climber/Vitalii Bashkatov), 32 (The Eden Project/David Hughes), 32 (Corpse Flower/Andrei Medvedev), 32 (pitcher plant/Decha Thapanya), 32 (The British Museum/Claudio Divizia), 33 (Gentoo penguin/Alexey Seafarer), 33 (swallow nest/Viesturs Jugs), 36 (girl on school bus/Monkey Business Images), 36 (shower/VaLiza), 36 (washing face/J2R), 36 (washing hands/karnavalfoto), 41 (salami/Nattika), 41 (grilled chicken/Moving Moment), 41 (tin tuna/Asier Romero), 44 (tuna salad/Jacek Chabraszewski), 44 (colourful cupcakes/Ruth Black), 45 (ghost/Joe Prachatree), 45 (boy asleep on bus/unguryanu), 46 (blacksmith/grafvision), 46 (pony/Andy Lidstone), 47 (compass/Olga Popova), 55 (sport figures/Iconslow), 57 (cheese making/stockfour), 57 (moon surface/HelenField), 57 (hurdler/ostill), 58 (accordion/RemarkEliza), 58 (waves/Kelly Headrick), 62 (shopping centre/ Lukasz Pajor), 62 (supermarket/06photo), 62 (school kids/Monkey Business Images), 62 (hospital/Spiroview Inc), 68 (battered sausage and chips/Richard M Lee), 68 (scotch eggs/D. Pimborough), 68 (fried chicken/dolphfyn), 72 (Golden Gate Bridge in San Francisco/Lucky-photographer), 72 (Tower Bridge/JuliaST), 78 (driver/Monkey Business Images), 78 (scientist/Gorodenkoff), 78 (shopping/ Dmitry Kalinovsky), 78 (cabin crew/Sorbis), 78 (barber/Basyn), 78 (mechanic/ Dmitry Kalinovsky), 78 (musician/Eugenio Marongiu), 78 (directors chair/ RomeoLu), 78 (spider/Sebastian Janicki), 80 (emojis/Carboxylase), 84 (coconut drink/apiguide).